Accountability in schools

edited by
Tyrrell Burgess

ACCOUNTABILITY IN SCHOOLS

Published by Longman Industry and Public Service Management, Longman Group UK Ltd, Westgate House, The High, Harlow, Essex CM20 1YR, UK.
Telephone: (0279) 442601
Fax: (0279) 444501

First published 1992

A catalogue record for this book is available from the British Library

ISBN 0-582-09002 4

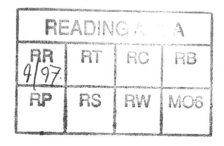

Printed and bound in Great Britain by
Biddles Ltd, Guildford and King's Lynn

Contents

Contributors

Michael Armstrong is headteacher of Harwell County Primary School, Oxfordshire

John Bazalgette is Director, The Grubb Institute

Tyrrell Burgess is Professor in the Philosophy of Social Institutions at the Polytechnic of East London

Michael Day is Chairman of the Commission for Racial Equality

Del Goddard is Chief Adviser, London Borough of Enfield

Susan Heightman is a parent and teacher at Tolworth Girls' School, Surrey

Gordon Lister is Chief Executive, Cambridgeshire County Council

Duncan McReddie is a county councillor in Cleveland

Jack Morrish is Chairman of Governors of a primary school and has been chairman or vice-chairman of the education committee in Northamptonshire and Hounslow

Pat Petch is Chairman of Governors of Stanley Junior School, London Borough of Richmond upon Thames

Maggie Pringle is Headteacher of Holland Park School, Kensington

Robin Richardson is Director, The Runnymede Trust

Jaki Stewart is a teacher at The Willows School, Hillingdon

Michael Stoten is Executive Director of Education and Libraries, London Borough of Kensington and Chelsea

Christine Webb is Head of English at Swakeley's School, Hillingdon

Acknowledgements

We are grateful to the following for permission to reproduce copyright material:

Faber & Faber, 1988, *Moon Wings* from *Moon Whales* by Ted Hughes; Brent Education Department, 1990 for extracts from *Drum, Talk and Drub* and *Children's Self-Worth Poems*; Sarsen Press, 1989, for 'Little Girl to School' by Bill Allchin, in *A Turmoil of Fragile Hearts*.

1 Introduction

1.1 Accountability with confidence

Tyrrell Burgess

The object of this book is to help to restore confidence to education. In recent years, there have been unprecedented 'initiatives', culminating in reform legislation, from central government. The stated object of the reform has been the improvement of 'standards'; the method, a combination of increased central control, particularly of the curriculum, and greater 'accountability' elsewhere. Its immediate consequence, however, has been to spread alarm, uncertainty, bewilderment and depression through the service. Low morale is not universal but it is common, among teachers, heads, governors, local authority members and officers, inspectors and even civil servants and Ministers. Parents have become used to hearing of their increased 'powers' while finding that the means by which these are to be exercised are dubious and ineffective.

It is time to take stock of the new balance of powers and duties and to make sense of new accountabilities. This the book does by giving accounts of the confident exercise of these responsibilities by good practitioners. It does not offer either complaints about 'policy' or demands for more 'resources'. Instead it shows how everyone in education can use personal capacities, qualities and experience to make the system and the individual's place within it work for the continuing benefit of children and young people.

Importantly, it recognises the traditional notion of 'partnership' in the service. No practitioner works alone: all depend on the work of others. The book reflects this understanding in the mode of its production. All the papers were written first for scrutiny at a working conference at Robinson College, Cambridge, in September 1991[1]. They were revised in the light of discussion there. The result is not 'the book of the conference' but a collection of statements distilling general experience, not just the practice of individuals, however successful. It has a shared and consistent approach and purpose. It is addressed to individuals working in education and to concerned parents. It may be especially attractive as a text for the innumerable in-service courses now available, for teachers, governors, officers and others.

One of the unhappy, and perhaps unintended, consequences of central initiatives is that since 1988 the idea has been growing that it is the Secretary of State who does everything in education — worse, that nothing is to be done unless he does it. The impression given is of restless activity at Waterloo, occasioned by torpor or worse elsewhere. The public may not quite have grasped that much of this impression is an illusion: most of the recent 'changes', for example, in the National Curriculum — like financial 'cuts' in the past — are to proposals, not to reality, so that things are actually going on much as before. The typical consequence of onerous experiment, as with assessments, has been a retreat towards the familiar.

It is clearly time to recall the great truth that education is a personal service which succeeds or fails with individuals, not with systems, and to notice that fortunately powers and duties are still widely distributed, so that all those responsibilities which bear directly upon individual children and young people are still held elsewhere than at the centre.

The duty to see that children are educated rests, not with any public authority, but with parents. What is more, they are still required to secure that this education is suitable to each individual child's age, ability and aptitude and even 'to any special educational needs he may have'. This is a serious duty. The provision made by the public authorities may make that duty easier or harder to perform but cannot remove it. The obligation on parents, through all and any changes that take place, is to secure that the system (whatever else it does) responds to the individual requirements of their children.

Each school — that is the governing body, professionally advised by the head and staff — still has to determine its own curriculum. This must be 'balanced and broadly based', it must 'promote the spiritual, moral, cultural, mental and physical development of pupils' and separately (and unrealistically) 'of society', and it must prepare pupils for adult life. Each governing body has to state the 'aims of the curriculum' (having taken into account the 'policy' of the local authority). It is the head of the school who is responsible for both determining and organising the curriculum, in the light of the law, the governors' 'aims' and the authority's 'policy'.

Again, the head's duty is a serious one. It has not been removed or diminished by the National Curriculum. Indeed, the law makes it entirely clear that a school's 'basic' curriculum includes and does not simply comprise the National Curriculum and religious education. Whatever the Secretary of State may order as to attainment targets, programmes of study and assessment arrangements, he is expressly forbidden to order how much time should be devoted to any of it. It is for the head to determine and organise a balanced, broad and individually responsive curriculum, using what is helpful in the National Curriculum and mitigating what is a hindrance.

As for local administration, it is still the duty of the local authority to see that there are enough schools for the children in its area. It has never had to provide these schools itself. It has been able to buy places in private schools and in schools maintained by other authorities; it has been empowered to maintain schools provided by private bodies, like churches. It must inspect any school it does maintain and it has many other duties — towards those with special educational needs, in curriculum policy, for finance and so on. Even if 'opting out' became general (for which the present level of bribery seems insufficient), the authorities' duties would still be serious. Important questions about the functioning of the authority itself (that is the members acting corporately) and of its professional administration (the statutory chief officer and his staff) remain: these are not to be settled once and for all, but need consistent attention.

It is important to recognise how stable the statutory distribution of powers and duties in education remains. The 1988 Act is a 'reform' Act: it does not replace other legislation. It cannot be read in isolation, but must take into account other Acts, including the basic Act of 1944, which established a rational and humane system of educational administration.

Even now, however, the law does not cover everything. Indeed it does not cover some of the most important things — like the relationship between the individual child and a teacher and the nature of a teacher's professional responsibility. The folly of trying to legislate for these things has not (yet?) been contemplated. Teachers are professional people, in that they maintain a relationship with a client (the pupil) in which the interests of the client are paramount; they have knowledge, experience and qualifications which they place at the client's service and they exercise individual judgement in the solution of a client's problems. They act in accordance with a set of values, so that professional conduct is ethical conduct. They are self-managing, accept responsibility for their own quality and keep themselves up to date. In short, they exercise authority within their sphere of service. They take all these responsibilities, not only singly but corporately in institutions — the schools.

The education service, then, is an interlocking set of statutory powers and duties, and non-statutory responsibilities. It can work effectively and develop creatively only if people grasp their responsibilities and act. It will collapse if they simply wait to be told what to do or do only what they are told. Equally, it is desirable that such action is fruitful, apt and free from harm, something that can best be secured not by direction and regulation, but through clear accountability.

The trouble is that people understand many different things by accountability. This is not a problem merely of definition. If it were, we could simply use another word. It is rather that accountability can be of many kinds: personal, professional, political, financial, managerial, legal, contractual. All these kinds of accountability are present in education, as is clear from the contributions which follow. It is worth sorting out which is which and thus trying to avoid making demands of one kind which can be made only of another.

The book begins with parents. Parents are a child's first educators. They have a natural and legal obligation to protect them and not to do them damage. In education law they must see that their children are educated. If they fail in this duty the local authority must prosecute them. If parents choose to educate their children at home, rather than at school, the authority must decide whether the education is full-time, efficient and suitable. In other words, parents are legally accountable to the authority (it can call them to account) for their duty to educate.

It is unlikely that this thought ever crosses the minds of most parents. As Susan Heightman makes clear, they feel accountable, but the accountability they feel is not legal but personal. Some parents may still have a lively idea of accountability to God, and a few may believe that they will render this account at the last trump. Most, however, have a substitute: they feel accountable to themselves, to their own consciences, to a set of moral values, to public opinion — represented by friends, other parents, a social circle — which creates shared expectations. In later chapters teachers describe how schools work to create a climate in which parental accountability, not to the schools, but to themselves, is enhanced.

Of these two kinds of accountability, it is interesting to note which is the more effective. The legal accountability is largely unknown: when parents fail, the legal sanctions do not work. It is not the law, the formal accountability, that makes parents talk to teachers, go to parents' evenings, worry about a choice of school or agonise over GCSE options. It is a parent's sense of accountability to what is personally and socially thought fitting. This will not be the last occasion on which we shall find ourselves contrasting personal responsibility and formal requirements.

The accountabilities of teachers are more various than those of parents, though their first duty is indeed parental: they are *in loco parentis*, and their authority, in school, is the same as that of a parent. A teacher must take proper care of pupils and is liable for negligence. Teachers also have a contractual accountability to their employers (the local authority or the governors of an aided school), they are liable for breach of contract and they are subject to disciplinary procedures. Their work may be inspected both by Her Majesty's inspectors and by inspectors from the local authority. There is no lack of formal and legal accountability, but although teachers may have a lively sense of this, it is not this that generally governs their daily performance.

The accountabilities that teachers habitually recognise are professional and managerial. The commitment to the client (the pupil), which lies at the heart of the characteristics of a professional person, is recognised, not just by Jaki Stewart and the teachers in this collection but by all teachers. That this extends to parents, up to and beyond compulsory school age, is evident in reports and parents' evenings. Teachers, more than most professionals, include in this commitment a readiness to account for what they are doing. Professional accountability also implies standards, of qualification, training, practice and conduct, to which teachers subscribe. Professionals are judged by other professionals: they are accountable to their peers. One of the strengths of the inspectorate (both HMI and local) until now is that teachers have been ready to see them as fellow professionals. The sense of professional accountability among teachers acts like that of personal accountability in parents: it is the accountability that, with individuals, works. Legal and contractual accountabilities exist and can be used in extremes, but they are not what secures proper performance. Commitment to pupils and their parents, to the outcomes of training, to best practice and to ethical standards are more effective here.

In Michael Armstrong's paper there is a further development of this responsibility: an attempt to find ways of accounting for a pupil's learning and enabling the pupil to do so. This goes far beyond ticks and grades which reward most school work. It argues that the central activity of schools — learning — is itself accountable.

Managerial accountability has different purposes from the professional: it is institutional, not individual. Teachers are responsible not just for their own performance but, together, for the performance of the whole school. Accountability for this runs through the headteacher. The chart in Christine Webb's paper (p. 44) sums up a familiar management organisation. In it, people have specified tasks and are accountable to someone for their exercise. Teachers, heads of year, heads of department and faculty, senior teachers, deputies and heads all recognise some further person, or persons, to whom they answer. Such accountability has institutional purposes. It makes possible the devising and working out of 'policy' — whether that derives from the head and staff or from the governing body. It is the means by which the head carries effective responsibility for the organisation, management and discipline of the school and accounts for this to the governors and the local authority. It is a means of control and direction. It is the form of accountability best understood in the world at large. All teachers recognise and accept it — without on the whole weakening their sense of professional accountability. Indeed the successful marrying of the two forms is what characterises the profession of teaching.

Headteachers have all the accountabilities of teachers, and more. It is through them that the accountability of schools is expressed. They answer to local authorities, governors and parents. The forms of their accountability are professional, managerial and semi-political. Not much needs to be added on the professional and managerial, except, perhaps, to point out that managerially the head answers both to the governors and to the local authority, and that since the introduction of local management of schools managerial includes financial.

A head's accountability to parents is different from the forms discussed hitherto. I have characterised it as semi-political. At the annual meeting which governors must have with parents, the parents may question the exercise of functions not only of the governors and the local authority but also of the headteacher, and they may pass resolutions on the head's activities. The obligation to explain and justify one's actions to those affected by them is a characteristic of political accountability — but it lacks the further characteristic of revocability. The head is not appointed by the parents and cannot be dismissed by them. Hence 'semi-political'.

It is worth noting here that whereas managerial accountability is possible, and indeed normal, without political accountability, it is hard to think of the latter without the former. Managerial accountability is a tool of the political, and we shall see later that political accountability becomes problematical if the managerial is lacking.

We saw earlier that inspection was one of the ways in which teachers and heads are held accountable. Inspection offers a professional judgement on the work of a school, first for those who work in it, second for those publicly responsible — the governors, the local authority and the Secretary of State — and third, through publication, for parents and the public at large. Inspectors' reports have traditionally not commented on individuals but have been concerned rather with the performance of the whole institution.

There are two ways of conducting an inspection. The first is to find answers to a series of questions: what does the school seek to do? Is this worth doing? Is it done well? This has hitherto been the approach of HMI. It enhances accountability by giving an independent view of the school's own account of itself. The second method is to arrive at the school with a checklist and tick off the extent to which the school matches it. This has become the recent tendency, even among HMI. It is an instrument, not so much of accountability, as of control. It replaces independent judgement about what a school is trying to do with pressure on the school to do what someone else wants. Del Goddard's paper explores the extent to which different approaches to inspection serve the desirable end of enhancing quality. It works best when it is part of the way in which a school reviews and accounts for its work — and 'contracting out' inspections will add to the challenge for schools to find ways of making them effective instruments of accountability.

There are no parts of the education service which have been untouched by recent reforms, but few have been affected so much and so problematically as governing bodies. Both their composition and functions have been greatly changed, and unlike most other parts of the service they have had no settled habits of action, no conventions of conduct, which remain apt in their new situation. As Pat Petch suggests, governing bodies are still finding their way.

In county and voluntary schools there have been new kinds of governors, elected directly by parents and teachers. In grant-maintained schools the whole governing body is 'new'. The question immediately arises as to how far the parent and teacher governors are representative, how far they are to report back to those who elected them. The answer seems clear: they are governors, like any other. They have no special duty to reflect the views of their electors, though they cannot and need not suppress the knowledge of those that they have. A governing body is accountable to parents through its annual report and annual meeting: parent governors have no additional and separate accountability. Governors do well to remember that they have no special standing as individuals: a governing body can only act corporately and by due process in accordance with its articles of government. An individual governor can act, by visiting a school, say, only if the whole governing body has given the authority to do so. The chairman normally has this delegated authority: other governors need to be given it explicitly.

Most of the powers and duties of governing bodies which are thought to have been conferred by recent legislation were inherent or implicit in earlier law, though in most places they had lacked use. Governors have always had serious responsibilities for the curriculum, finance, staff appointments and discipline. The merit of recent changes is that the responsibilities are clearly re-stated. In some instances the local authority, which had encroached on the governors' responsibilities, is now explicitly excluded.

The clear placing of responsibility, however, does not make it easier to determine how the responsibility should be exercised. The problem can be put quite simply: if governors are to do, on their own initiative and by their own action, all the things for which they are responsible, they, or many of them, would have to be full-time officials. This is clearly not intended, yet governors are clearly accountable. They are accountable annually to parents, to the local authority (for example for financial management, where if they fail the delegated responsibility can be withdrawn), to the Secretary of State, for incorporating the National Curriculum. How can they be accountable, if they do not actually do anything?

The answer lies in their securing performance by others. Governors are on the whole lay persons: what is done in school is done by professionals. The chief function of a governing body is to be the body to whom the professionals, the head and staff, are accountable. In this sense they stand proxy for the population at large — since it is clearly impossible for schools to account directly to the public, except in the most general way. For example, governors are responsible for the curriculum: they must have a statement of general aims. It is the headteacher who is responsible for determining, organising and delivering it, and must account to the governors for doing so. The governors are responsible for financial management, but it is the head who actually manages. The governors may cause a school to be inspected; they do not themselves inspect. My belief is that they would be wise to take the same view of appointments, giving up the farce of interviewing candidates in a large committee and putting themselves, instead, in a position where they can check the judgement and practice of the head in appointing staff.

There is an argument for this view of the governors' function which goes beyond the obvious one of avoiding an overload of work. It is that if a headteacher is accountable to the governors, accountability exists: if the governors usurp the headteacher's functions, they become largely unaccountable. The point was made starkly by the experience of the grant-maintained Stratford School: the governors sought to usurp the functions of the head, to exercise their responsibilities directly and not through professionals — and they became at once out of control, even of the Secretary of State.

The view being advanced here is that governors act best when they see themselves as the means through which a school is accountable. It is a semi-political accountability, in that they are required publicly to justify themselves to, but are not revocable by, the public. This rests upon the secure managerial, legal and financial accountability which we have already seen exists within schools.

The last body represented in this book is the local education authority. The authorities are the councils of shire counties, metropolitan districts and London boroughs. In each case, the authority is the council, that is, the members acting corporately. In exercising its functions, however, an authority must appoint and take the advice of an education committee, which must include additional members with a knowledge of education; and it must appoint a chief education officer or director of education. An authority presents itself to the public both through the elected members and through the professional officers. It is the members who are responsible: together they *are* the authority. It is on the whole the officers who act.

This division of function (which is similar to that in schools between governors and heads and in government between Ministers and civil servants) rests upon a constitutional scepticism about politicians and experts. In English local government there are no directly elected officials. The politicians are accountable to the public, but do not run the service; the officers who do this do not have the last word. Each is a check on the other. The object is to guard against the weaknesses of democracy — that politicians may act ignorantly or corruptly — and of bureaucracy — that officials may be overmighty. The strengths of the system are too often taken for granted: they are appreciated when it breaks down. In the 1940s and 1950s the danger was from authoritarian chief officers who were largely out of members' control. More recently, the danger has been from meddling members who have bullied through their personal and political fads. In most authorities the balance has been held.

It is in the local education authorities that the full range of accountabilities is clearly seen. The chief education officer or director of education is appointed by the council and is clearly accountable to it. Yet it is a statutory appointment, which gives it a more independent standing than those offices that the council itself decides should exist. Chief officers are personally accountable, in that if they act beyond their powers or those of the council they can be surcharged. They are professionals and have a professional accountability to standards of behaviour and practice. They owe a duty to the client — the council not just the majority party — and in that duty they exercise managerial and financial accountability. Even this is done in more than one way. The chief officer is managerially and financially accountable for the education department, in a way that is familiar in any large organisation, public or private. The same accountability for schools is exercised differently: here the chief officer has to work through headteachers, who are themselves professionals and, as we have seen, carry these accountabilities within the schools. This is emphasised by recent provisions for the local management of schools. It is far from the simple accountability of 'line management' and requires something more like leadership and less like administration.

All these complexities are treated in Michael Stoten's chapter, which also reflects the lively sense that a chief officer has of the object of the service — the education of children. It is hard to think of this commitment to the service of children and their parents in terms of direct accountability, but it is always there: it informs the sense of professional accountability and determines the way in which other accountabilities are exercised. Gordon Lister reinforces the point by describing how one authority seeks to ensure that whatever degree of independence individual schools may have in future, they will embrace it with confidence, so that the change may be productive and free from harm — to the pupils.

With elected members the range of accountabilities extends further. They are personally accountable in that they too can be surcharged if they act beyond their powers. They are financially accountable in that they have a fiduciary duty enforceable in the courts: they are trustees for public money, and their accounts are subject to audit. Above all, however, they are politically accountable. They are directly elected and can thus be recalled. This political accountability lies at the heart of English local government. The United Kingdom is a unitary state: the only sovereign power is the Queen in Parliament. Other bodies, like local authorities, can exercise only those powers that have been given to them by Parliament. Yet the authorities themselves are elected and thus have an accountability to their electorates. Until quite recently they also had, from Parliament, independent power to raise taxes (the rates) and this remains in an attenuated and controlled form with the community charge or poll tax. This means that though local authorities may be creatures of Parliament, they are not (like health authorities) creatures of a Secretary of State. They have their own electoral and financial legitimacy. They are not confined (as are health authorities) to carrying out the Secretary of State's policies within the sums of money which he makes available. A local education authority, for example, is required by law to have its own policy for the curriculum.

The evidence is that local authority members have a lively sense of political accountability. They know that they are revocable. This sense remains despite the well known threats to it, which include low turnouts at local elections, increasing control by central government and the dominant rigidities of party politics. This is because periodic elections are not the only form of political accountability, and not by any means the most effective, though others may depend upon them. Another form is the obligation, more or less persistently enforced by electors and tax payers, to explain and justify the authorities' actions all the time, not just at elections. The paper by McReddie and Morrish details the ways in which this is done. All rest on the accessibility of local members. They are available to individuals with a complaint or a request, they visit institutions, their proceedings, even in subcommittees, are public. They have the habit of consulting publicly on any major proposal. Political parties carry the danger that members may feel more accountable to them than to the electorate, but they have the advantage of providing an institutionalised source of criticism, ideas and knowledge. Local government, certainly compared with central government, is open. The detail of council decisions is a matter of report and comment in the local press.

This openness serves the political process too. Since committees and subcommittees are public, the professional service of officers is made available to the opposition parties as well as to the majority. Everyone sees the papers. Consequently the opposition in local government is much better informed than the opposition in Parliament, and even opposition councillors are better informed than most backbenchers of both sides in Parliament. Their day-to-day accountability to the public is made possible and enhanced.

The question which commonly arises is whether this accountability, which is visible and felt, can be effective when councillors are voluntary, part-time lay persons. Can they possibly be in 'control' and if not, can they be said to be accountable? Councillors themselves sometimes seek to explain what might seem to be an awkward position by saying that they, the council, make the policy, while officers implement it. This oversimplifies, indeed trivialises, a complex relationship. The attempt to enforce it in some city authorities, when the dominant party sought to 'control', to run the services day-to-day, to exclude opposition members from committees, to instruct officers, led quickly to the debauch of administration. The accountable function of councillors is not to run the service: that is the proper duty of officers. A representative body, like a council, and its committees, cannot govern or manage directly. Instead, it must watch and control the administration, publicise its actions, demand explanation and justification, and discipline professional failure. When they act in this way, the administration can be held daily accountable on behalf of the public. When councillors seek to do things themselves, they are effectively accountable to no-one.

Some councillors seek to defend this position on the ground that they have, after an election, a 'mandate' to pursue certain 'policies'. It is a temptation to a certain kind of politician (of any party) to put a lot of detail before an electorate and use electoral success to silence opposition to detailed acts, or even prevent their own second thoughts. The use of the 'mandate' in this way is a perversion and is recognised as such by electors who are entirely ready to oppose with vigour particular acts of a recently elected body. The purpose of general policy is to alert the officers of a council to the general principles on which their detailed performance will be judged. A change of political 'climate' following an election quickly communicates itself both to the administration and to the public. It is not necessary to try to enforce the 'implementation' of particular solutions to detailed problems on officers whose professional judgement is different.

This, if anything, is the lesson to be learned from this book. People in education, from the class teacher to the elected member, understand both the nature of accountability and the fact that it is expressed in many forms. They know they are accountable in many different directions and in many different ways. This variety may be implicit and hard to describe without thought, but it is not unclear. The various forms of accountability can be, and are, exercised with confidence. They are all better exercised, not in isolation, still less in confrontation, but in partnership. It is here, not in prescription, instruction and regulation that quality is to be found.

Note

[1]   The conference was sponsored by Action for Governors' Information and Training, the Association of Metropolitan Authorities, The Grubb Institute and the National Association of Head Teachers and Supported by the Department of Education and Science.

The Conference Steering Committee included John Bazalgette and Tyrrell Burgess (contributors to the present book), Ann Holt (AGIT) and Hilary Delyon (AMA), and its organiser was Tom Hinds (Hinds Education and Review). To him and to all the participants at the conference the contributors are very grateful.

2 The family and education

2.1 Parenthood

Susan Heightman

To begin at the beginning seems apt, but when does parenting begin? Is it at birth or before birth? In my family, even before the conception of our first child, Nick and I discussed whether we were ready to take on the new role as parents, and in those discussions a major responsibility was the education of the hoped-for child. When people have the real choice whether and when they will become parents, accountability seems a natural consequence. At my ante-natal classes I discovered that I was not alone in this. All the mothers-to-be were re-valuing their own education and life experiences and considering their roles in securing for their children what was best and what would bring them greatest happiness and security. This was an introspective and strangely vulnerable time. I remember reading anything that promised answers to questions about the needs of babies and children. I changed my diet, gave up smoking, meditated to increase the baby's oxygen supply, haunted the childcare shelves in bookshops and libraries and started buying women's magazines for the first time in my life. I felt accountable, I was happy but I was not confident. I had no experience within my family of sharing responsibility for younger children and I had received only the standard grammar school education, which did not acknowledge within the curriculum that the pupils would one day be parents. Thirty years later, after so much curriculum reform, many secondary schools still do not seriously attempt to explore parenthood in courses of study. The Elton Report on discipline in schools recommended that such courses should be taken by all children, but this does not seem to have had impact on the planners of the National Curriculum. Perhaps this is a reflection of the lack of respect our culture shows to the important role of being a parent: as a result school time is heavily weighted towards the learning of work-related skills and knowledge.

Fortunately for women, pregnancy is a time when many other caring and experienced adults give support — friends, family, doctors, nurses and even the chance-met stranger. They do so because you show your need for it and a preparedness to accept what is on offer. I suggest that it is important that parents continue to show an interest in receiving advice and support from others as their children move through the later stages of childhood and adolescence. There is considerable evidence from the work of voluntary groups and child charities that mutual support-groups can enable parents to help each other. Some children with serious learning, emotional or physical problems need adults (teachers and parents) who have developed special expertise and understanding. In-service training can help teachers in developing such skills but parents can possibly be most helped by sharing their experiences and understanding within self-help groups, which may in time become very effective learning networks.

The birth of Melissa, my first daughter, was a joyous event. In many respects, she came to a well resourced home and family; there were no external pressures of finance or accommodation, and her parents had been happily married for 10 years. I do not list these things because I believe they are a prerequisite for good parenting, but because I recognise that many loving parents have far fewer resources and therefore face additional challenges or burdens. A strong and caring society must find resources and structures that will be a safety net, supporting those parents in need of support, if all children, our society's most precious resource, are to be fully valued and developed. These resources can be created in the community but more than rhetoric is needed to put them in place. We must as members of society take a caring sense of responsibility for the well-being and behaviour of all children, not just our own.

One of the many choices Nick and I had taken together as potential parents was that I would continue my career as a teacher and Melissa would go to a childminder. I felt guilty about making that choice whilst at the same time I knew I would have felt unfulfilled if I had not returned to work. I took that decision in 1976, at a time when the majority of mothers stayed at home during their children's infant years. Today, 16 years later, most mothers are making the same choice as I did, against an economic background that puts greater pressure on them to continue to be wage earners. More women today are having to meet the potentially conflicting demands of two roles, employee and mother. They need the understanding and active support of the family and the employer if the conflict is to be managed and the needs of all — child, mother and employer — are to be recognised and met.

It is interesting to reflect on how I coped with that situation. Significantly, I shared my doubts with our childminder who helped me to explore them and accept the responsibility for my decision with confidence. Together, as a family, we planned to give Melissa 'her time'. At home, she was the focus of our attention when she was awake. We knew that she needed to grow up feeling valued, and that people only feel valued when you give them time. Giving time is a tangible proof of love which is more powerful than toys or sentimental words — not that we did not give her those too, as shown by the poem I wrote when she was 18 months.

A present for Melissa

On a busy day, each parcelled time off,
Separate from other spent minutes,
To find a gift for our baby daughter.
She needed a private house of her own
With tables and chairs that could perch
Safe in a tiny hand and become
The pieces of a doll-sized land.

The actions of the day sent
Daddy his way and Mummy mine.
Neither had confessed the planned
Extravagance, but both were blessed
To find exactly what each had in mind.
At the end of the working day both
Identical homes were unpacked by our
Laughing child, caught, delighted, unaware.
And we, amazed parents, wondered too
At that mirrored moment reflecting true
The subtle union that our lives share.

During Melissa's years of infancy, we shared with her childminder, a most admirable and loved friend, control over Melissa's environment. As the months passed and she grew along the perfect curve for her birth weight, began to speak and walk early, was alert and generally jolly, we became more confident parents. Everything was happening as it should according to all those books I had bought during the pregnancy. Five years later with my second child, Eleanor, we were to experience the doubt and worry of parents who know that their child needs medical care and surgery, to correct eyesight and hearing difficulties. But fortunately, by 1981, we were more confident to cope with that situation. We had learnt to question the system, and could use our GP, hospital specialists and educational specialists to advise us in our shared role in helping Eleanor. If being a parent is the single most significant learning experience in your life, then it is not surprising that it is easier second time around to overcome difficulties. I am sure that 'first-time' parents need a special kind of understanding and help from education, welfare and health services. New parents need to talk through how to respond to their child's needs if they are to arrive at confident conclusions. Too often 'experts' present one neatly packaged solution to parents without engaging in real dialogue. Such solutions may not be understood or fully accepted. As a result, the solution will not be enacted with understanding or commitment, and neither child nor parents will benefit.

Melissa's introduction to school was gradual and very happy. She attended a local playgroup for two short sessions a week and grew in confidence to do things (especially with water), either alone or with her new-found friends. The two sessions were extended to three, then four, and Melissa's conversations were as full of references to her playgroup activities as our kitchen walls were covered with her artistic achievements. I never met her playgroup leaders, and even today I regret that I did not personally know the people who gave Melissa such a wonderful introduction to school.

Within four months we discovered that Nick's job was to take us to Brussels. I felt anxious about the move but Melissa was as furiously angry as a child of nearly three can be. Underneath the anger was fear. She was in control of her present world which was full of loved people — her grandparents, the entire family of her childminder, her local friends, her teachers at the playgroup. Melissa's trust in us had been as total as the trust that most three-year-olds place in their parents. Now we had placed that trust under pressure. She could not really understand why a loving Mummy and Daddy were doing this to her. Because her trust in us was dented, her trust in other previously loved adults was very obviously withdrawn. She became increasingly Mummy and Daddy dependent. At the time I can remember making the mistake of thinking 'least said soonest mended'. We tended not to talk about the move in front of her in an attempt to minimise for Melissa what was happening. We let the momentum of events carry us forward without truthfully facing the difficulties being experienced by our child. Children know when you are dodging the issue, and it never works. If the parent will not, for whatever reason, face up honestly to the problems and challenges of life, how can they look for strength and trust from their children?

After three unhappy months in Brussels, our confidence as adults returned and only then did we begin to help our child. We had honestly to accept the responsibility for choosing to come to Brussels and we had to explain to Melissa all our reasons for making that choice. I am sure that much of what we said to Melissa was over the head of a three-year-old but she seemed to understand the attempt at honesty and agreed that if she was still not liking Brussels after she was four then we would come back to England to live.

We were faced with a choice of four schools for Melissa's infant education: a state Belgian school with instruction in French and Flemish, an independent Belgian school with instruction in French and two independent international schools where the language of instruction was English. The opportunity was there for our child to become fluent in another language at an early age but we had no difficulty in deciding that we wanted Melissa to attend an English-speaking school. As with so many choices that parents have to make about education for their children, there are no right or wrong decisions. The point is to have confidence in the decision taken and to devote energy and committed concern to helping the child to relate well to the new school rather than to doubt the wisdom of the choice. Such doubts, continually voiced, can make the child insecure and even negative.

A parent of young children ought to accept responsibility for the development of a child's principles and attitudes, including attitudes to school, teachers, children and other adults. How can a child work enthusiastically for teachers whom the parent continually criticises? Can a child contribute wholeheartedly to the life of a school which in family discussions is endlessly described in negative terms? It will help the child in so many ways if the parents are seen to be talking problems through in a constructive and controlled manner with teachers. There is a considerable difference between negotiating on behalf of a child, and telling the teachers what is wrong with them and the school.

Melissa's early years of full-time education were largely problem-free. Her only failing seemed to be a tendency to disappear when it was time to tidy up the classroom! We attempted to put that right by insisting that she tidied up her bedroom at home. We had previously taken the easy way out by tidying up for her and had only succeeded in teaching her that it was acceptable for her to leave tidying up to other people. Schools are a very useful check on whether you are helping a child to move towards the proper level of independent responsibility. Parents may mistakenly extend the child's infant dependency beyond infant years because it seems the loving thing to do. Mother and Father do everything for the child as proof of their love. But love is not simply giving: it is giving and withholding at the right time. If the parent is always and only giving, the child grows up with the idea that love is a dependent relationship, not an equally responsible, shared relationship. People prefer to see themselves as independent, responsible and loving adults. Whether they become that depends on how parents and schools work together to lead children to a growing sense of independent responsibility. Teachers can give parents a very useful 'outsider's' view of how their child is progressing along the path to adult responsibility if the parent will truly listen to the teacher's perception of their child's attitudes and behaviour. Parents are responsible to their children to do the job of parenting well. They are also responsible to society. The needs of the child and of society need not conflict; they are complementary. A parent may help children to read, helping them to enter a new world of independent learning where they can pick up a book and discover for themselves. This is, at the same time, a valuable contribution to society, of direct benefit, first in the classroom and then in working life.

The Education Act, 1944, places upon parents the legal responsibility to ensure that their children are educated, and most parents do this through schools. The parent may not leave the decision of whether to attend or not to the child, nor may the parent keep the child away from school to suit some domestic convenience. These matters are fundamental to parental accountability. In schools where truancy and absence figures are high the parents must take their share of the responsibility: it is not enought to blame the school. Equally it is the parent's responsibility to send the child to school in a fit state to learn. Common sense and the findings of research both suggest that a child who has not eaten breakfast, or who has been up watching videos until the early hours of the morning, will not be a fully effective learner.

One of the most important ways in which parents can contribute to their child's education is by listening to the child. I can still remember Melissa and Eleanor's six-year-old burblings about their lessons, their friends, their successes, their disasters and the endless questions. Sometimes we were tired or selfish and did not give enough attention but at least we did not silence them. It is important to give children undivided listening attention for at least some time every day. In this way a parent will be taking part in the children's learning, will discover where they are having difficulties and can step in to protect their self-esteem. When Eleanor first attended infant school on our return to England, she was placed in a mixed-age class with children who were nearly 18 months older. Eleanor is small for her age but she is a bright, expressive child who had not previously experienced difficulties in making friends or keeping up with the work of the class. Suddenly she found keeping up with 'the big children' hard in a number of ways. She felt overwhelmed and became anxious. Her end-of-day chats about school became unenthusiastic, she lost her bubbly joy in life and began to have disturbed nights. I went to the school to discuss the situation with her teacher who had doubts about the mixed-age system and was obviously concerned at the difficulty of meeting the very varied needs of 28 children with an age range of two years. I went on to the headteacher who had no such doubts but who told me I was an over-anxious mother. I then changed Eleanor's school. We knew that we had to act because we were confident in our understanding of our child. Parents cannot act with decisive confidence if they have not spent time understanding and listening to their child.

As the child matures parents need to listen more attentively both to the child and to the teachers. Transition from one school to the next is a critical time. Indeed it can cause considerable soul searching and stress. One of the many features that I valued about my children's school in Brussels was that the infant, junior and secondary schools were integrated on one site and that transition was managed in a planned, well informed way. Had we stayed in Brussels, Melissa would not have had to worry about which secondary school she should go to or whether she would like it when she got there. We returned to England when Melissa was nine, which meant that she was still trying to fit into her new junior school while surrounded by classmates who had begun the serious debate about whether to sit the 11-plus exam for the local grammar school, attempt the entrance exam for an independent school or go to one of the local secondary schools. Melissa was out of step with her class because she had been in full-time education from the age of three, had been taught in class sizes of 18 and in Brussels had been placed in a class that was ahead of her chronological age. Her form teacher and the headmaster of her new junior school could not see an easy solution to the problem that Melissa posed by being 'very advanced'. The local education authority had a policy of keeping children with their age group, irrespective of academic ability or intellectual development, which they justified by giving priority to emotional maturity and development.

We finally decided to act on one of the suggestions made by Melissa's headmaster and placed Melissa at a local independent school. There she would be in an educational environment that had some similarities to her experience in Brussels and she would be able to transfer to the senior department at 11 without another change of school. Melissa, who was still missing her school in Brussels, did not want to change schools again but she was sufficiently open to persuasion to convince us that she was finding her present lessons rather unchallenging.

Increasing mobility has implications for the education of children. Moving home to a new country or education authority places children in different systems, with transition at different ages, which makes transfer from school to school complex and sometimes difficult. But whatever the circumstances, parents need to be well informed about their children's ability, how they learn and special aptitudes or difficulties. Parents also need to understand in some detail the different provision offered by schools if they are to exercise choice with understanding. This demands commitment from parents and openness from schools. At the age of 11 the children's opinions are also important, since it is unlikely that they will be happy at and committed to a school that they do not wish to attend. The growing influence of friends is another factor that the wise parent will attempt to 'manage' by encouraging the children to think through choices and express opinions. The silenced child who feels misunderstood is much more vulnerable to the pressure and the influence of friends.

There remains the issue of how parents can best respond when they have no choice about their child's school because only one 'unsatisfactory' school is available, when they do not feel satisfied with any of the schools or when they cannot place their child at the school of their first or even second preference. In this situation they have three options: to send the child to a boarding school (an option open to a tiny percentage of the population), to educate the child at home, or to make the best of the school that is available. I believe that making the best of a school is the best strategy, irrespective of whether the school is a first choice or the only option and whether the school is a state or private school. No school can be the perfect organisation that will meet, unaided, the individual educational needs of each and every child. No parent should, with complacency, just leave it to the school to educate. Sadly some parents believe that it is enough to pay school fees or fill in the choice forms for the local education authority. Wise parents know that if they are to make the best of their child's school, they should build relationships with the teachers. Supportive and interested parents will seek to know about the work their children are doing, at school and for homework. Schools are required to make syllabuses and schemes of work available to parents and they want the parents to work with them in ensuring that homework is done.

Many parents seem confident about playing a part in the education of their very young children but step back from doing so when the children are older. Teenagers asked about their parents' views often reply that their parents do not take any interest in them any more. Perhaps this happens because the parents, faced with so many changes in subject content and teaching methods, lose confidence, are afraid to ask questions and to seem unknowledgeable. The result is that parents cease to have contact with children's learning. In fact, there is no need for parents to know everything. Children need to see that their parents are still learning too and still asking questions. I know nothing of any significance about physics, but that does not stop me from asking Melissa what she has learnt. So the child tells the story of her learning; the child becomes the teacher of the parent and grows in self-esteem. I cannot play a musical instrument or read music, but I will listen to Eleanor playing, show appreciation and take her to concerts. The varied financial and domestic situation of parents gives wide choice to some, in the ways in which they can extend their children's learning, and much less choice or sadly almost none to others. But limited financial resources can be compensated for, if the child is a member of the local library, which is free, or if through membership of church and community organisations, the parent and child have access to the richness of community activities. Schools can help parents get in touch with such organisations: they can be at the centre of community life. It is right, too, for parents to have a view about public provision for education. Political decisions may be taken to reduce public expenditure on some items and shift responsibility onto parents. For some parents, filling the gap this creates is very difficult financially. Others have not accepted the time commitment called for, or are unaware of the significance of the changes that have taken place. Parents with sufficient self confidence can consider what their children's needs are and, if they feel that these are not being met, can put pressure on those responsible. There has been considerable discussion about standards in education and the need for schools to feel answerable to parents. None of the recent legislation, however, significantly increases a parent's real control. There is no maximum class size or minimum expenditure on texts and materials. Parent governors are well placed to lobby for such things.

When it came to Melissa's time to choose her subjects for GCSE we entered into an extended debate with her. All the usual thorny issues emerged: friends making different choices; too little time for her to do all the subjects she wanted; and unfortunate timetable clashes. We had to be prepared to listen very attentively as Melissa tried to work it out for herself, and we had to be skilled in asking the right kind of open but answerable questions. We visited her school and sought the advice of her teachers who seemed as interested to understand our perceptions of Melissa's situation and reactions as we were to know theirs. We sensed a real parent-teacher partnership that valued Melissa as an individual and respected what each 'partner' had to contribute.

Recent debates have sadly failed to acknowledge the very good relationships that exist between most parents and teachers, ignoring recent findings that over 85 per cent of parents were satisfied with their children's schools. Parents and teachers do well to begin from the position of mutual trust. Both need to give an account of their perception of the child to each other rather than demand explanations or hurl recriminations. Where either senses failure this should be honestly acknowledged. If the parent really cannot correct a poor learning experience with the help of the staff, the parent can and should use structures such as the governing body to put the situation right.

At the final 'options evening' Melissa's teachers were confident that it was important for her to find her own answers, make her own choices and take her own risks. There may be no right answers, but there are ways of making the answer come out right if the individual is committed to the decision taken. As we watched our daughter going through this process of independent choice, we realised that it was a significant step in growing up, a step that was more significant than those smaller earlier steps like going to town with friends or taking responsibility for her younger sister. She was moving from childhood into being an adult through exercising her own choices that would affect her future life. She was looking forwards and outwards, and we had to give her room to achieve that transition. As parents we both had our own ideas about what subjects we would like Melissa to choose but we had to trust her judgement and show that her choice would have our respect simply because it was her choice. She did not have to fulfil our expectations, but to know herself and come to her decision. In taking part in the discussions with Melissa's teachers and in listening to Melissa's thoughts about what learning she valued and why, I learnt a great deal myself, about Melissa, and her educational experiences.

In recalling conversations that I have had over the years with other parents about what they have wanted from education and schools for their children, it seems that their fundamental requirements have been remarkably similar. They have wanted schools where learning was truly valued and where staff and pupils together shared and acted on a coherent set of beliefs. Schools like that do work well for all children. Equally, if parents are to play their full part in the development and education of their children, they must be strongly committed, they must value learning and, within the home, they must hold and act on a coherent set of beliefs. As parents, surely we owe our children no less than we would expect of any good school.

3 Teaching and learning

3.1 Rendering an account

Michael Armstrong

I want to write about the question which has dominated my thinking about education for the past 10 years. The question is this: how do we render an account of children's learning? How do we describe or represent that learning to ourselves as educators, whether we are parents, teachers or administrators? I use the word learning in a double sense, to define both a process and an accomplishment, as when we speak of a scholar's learning. There is a further question: how do we account for learning? I am not sure how far this second question is answerable; in any case I am not competent to answer it. My purpose is description rather than explanation.

The paper is in two parts. The first part presents a speculative account of a fragment of one child's learning. I intend it as a paradigm. I want to claim that significant learning is always open to interpretation in this way, whatever the subject matter, whoever the child. I also want to imply that the promotion of learning of this quality is the chief reason for a school's existence. The second part of the paper addresses certain issues which arise out of the paradigm. All of them touch on the question of accountability. The second part may therefore seem more directly relevant to the theme of this book than the first, but the way in which we answer questions of accountability depends on the kind of account that we give of children's learning. This is where I begin.

A case of learning: poetic narrative at the age of nine

Moon Whales is a collection of poems by Ted Hughes, lavishly illustrated by Chris Riddell.[1] Among the poems, which catalogue the disconcerting landscape of the moon, with its wayward flora and fauna, is one entitled Moon-Wings.

> *Moon-Wings*
>
> Unexpectedly descending things
> Are these moon-wings.
>
> Broad, soft, silent and white
> And like a huge barn owl's is their flight.

They veer and eddy and swoop.
They loop the alarming loop.

No head or limbs or body — just wings,
A pair pounces down on you and clings —

You feel them trying to grow
Into your shoulder blades, then they flap and you go

You go you go you go —
Where or which way you can never know.

High over goggling faces you are swung —
And just as unexpectedly suddenly flung

Down to the ground — after flying
Nine or ten miles without trying.

Then the wings just whirl off
With a sort of whiffling laugh.

One day last term I read Moon-Wings, and a second poem from the same collection, to my class of eight- and nine-year-old children as a stimulus for their own writing. We talked for a few minutes about the poems, and about the moon, after which the children began to write. A majority wrote stories which bore no more than a passing resemblance to the poems which I had read. Carley Still, however, a nine-year-old, chose to model herself on Moon-Wings. By the end of the morning she had handed me the poem that follows, with a characteristically shy smile which I never quite know what to make of. It is entitled Moon Wing Boots. (In transcribing the original I have observed Carley's own line endings but I have revised the original punctuation in the light of a discussion which I had with Carley about this.)

Moon Wing Boots

They fly in the air all the time they
never come down day or night they stay
in the air flying flying everywhere never
stop to say Hello never sit never walk stay
in the air all the time. When it's dark
they go round to fetch little boys and
girls. They slowly put the shrinking
boot into their backs. It hurts
at first then the wings start to flap
you go up into the air. It's fun at first but then
it gets a bit horrible. Then you look back the wings
are coming out of your back you see the boot coming
out you hear the horrible noises it makes
slivery sliding shivering shaking slowly slivering

all night long then you feel the wings come
out. You are a thousand feet from earth
you look up the wings are flapping away
you look down you're falling fast
you can't stop BANG you're dead.

Moon Wing Boots might be taken as a critical reading of the poem
by Ted Hughes. Or it might be seen as a reworking of Hughes's
imagery, a reconstruction of his vision. Or as a retelling — one more
event in 'that slow piling one on top of the other of thin transparent
layers which', according to the German philosopher and critic Walter
Benjamin, 'constitutes the most appropriate picture of the way in
which the perfect narrative is revealed through the layers of a variety
of retellings'. Benjamin's essay 'The Storyteller', from which these
remarks are taken, makes fascinating reading for anyone who is
interested in children as storytellers, although it never mentions
education.[2] But I think it's best to delay the confrontation of the two
poems until Moon Wing Boots has been observed more closely.

I start with the boots. Carley has drawn them above her title and
again below the poem's devastating conclusion. They hardly look
violent. If anything they remind me of the roller boots which Carley
and her friends ask to bring to school on the last day of term —
traditionally a day given to games and toys — so that they can career
around the playground showing off their skills and, not altogether
incidentally, the boots themselves. In class one child was reminded of
Perseus's winged boots — we'd been studying the story of Perseus
earlier in the year. In any case these boots, at a glance, promise
adventure, a kindly magic.

If so the promise is deceptive, undermined already in the opening
lines.

'They fly in the air all the time they
never come down day or night they stay
in the air flying flying everywhere never
stop to say Hello never sit never walk stay
in the air all the time.'

The power of flight has deprived the boots of their function. These
boots weren't made for walking. Momentarily in the first three lines
ceaseless flight seems full of wonder and charm in its boundlessness,
echoed in the inner rhymes — 'air . . . air . . . everywhere . . .' — and
in the repetition of 'flying flying'. But immediately the charm is
questioned — 'never stop to say Hello never sit never walk'.

'Never stop to say Hello' is one of those moments, endearing and
therefore often misunderstood, at which a young writer's naivety
opens up significant possibilities which are beyond the scope of
writers later in their development. We smile, but not entirely with the
writer or the poem. For 'never stop to say Hello' is not a charming

but, rather, a terrifying expression. It suggests that these boots, for all the boundless excitement which they promise, are dangerously detached from human concerns. Suddenly the thought that they 'never sit never walk' implies constraint rather than opportunity. When the opening words return — 'stay in the air all the time' — they come with very different colouring, a change marked by the substitution of the oppressive word 'stay' for the liberating word 'fly'. (There is a question to be asked about a young writer's intentions in respect of this style of interpretation. I will not try to answer it here directly. I will only say that I don't think that the interpretation of 'stay' and 'fly' which I have just proposed infringes the legitimate bounds of interpretation as far as Carley's poem is concerned.)

Now the terror enters, as if in a second stanza or chapter. To the aimlessness of ceaseless flight is added a threatening note, a kind of purpose although the purpose is without reason, unexplained. 'When it's dark they go round to fetch little boys and girls.' With these words the poem moves into the world of fairy tale, but, as it turns out, a fairy tale deprived of its 'liberating magic', as Benjamin describes it in the essay I have cited. This is the first of two moments of transition in the poem. Appropriately it is introduced by the only subordinate clause in the entire piece — 'when it's dark' — which signals the commencement of the narrative. Previously we have heard no more than the announcement of a subject. The dark purpose now animates a plot.

It's 'dark', they 'fetch'. Juxtaposed in the one sentence these two words hint at a sinister design which the following sentence horribly confirms — 'they slowly put the shrinking boot into their backs'. (I will note here in passing that when I reached this point for the first time in Carley's poem I didn't trust myself to have read the word 'shrinking' correctly and paused to ask her if that was what she meant. She did.) It's possible that Carley has derived 'shrinking' in some way from Ted Hughes's 'alarming loop'. What is certain is that the word condenses and then brings wonderfully to life an almost unmanageable image. If you try to visualise what happens you are heading for confusion. But 'shrinking' is so powerful a term in this context that there is no need to look beyond it. It is the most important word in the poem, anticipating and later triggering the disgust with which the boot's extrication of itself is experienced. The sounds that then overwhelm the poem are felt here for the first time — 'slowly . . . shrinking . . . backs'.

'It hurts at first then the wings start to flap', as if in the excitement of becoming airborne the pain is forgotten. Like so much else in this poem the words 'at first' are about to prove doubly deceptive, but first comes the moment of take-off and it is at this point in the poem that the second transition occurs. So far the victims have been 'little boys and girls', unnamed objects of the boots' unmotivated violence. With take-off the narrator brings them alarmingly closer. The third person pronoun vanishes, giving place to 'you' — 'you go up into the air'. This shift is no accident. From here on the third person never reappears. In the manuscript of the poem this second transition is marked by a change in the length of the handwritten lines. It is tempting to read this lengthening of the line as a recognition of the change that has come over the poem but perhaps this is to breach the limits of interpretation. At any rate, from this point until the end the poem abandons the fairy-tale genre and becomes a form of nightmare. As in many nightmares, the victim is both the narrator and the narrated subject. Is 'you' me or not me? The answer is, it might be. The transition occurs in mid-sentence. Once the sentence on either side of the lengthened line is put together a further implication of the change of person appears. 'It hurts at first then the wings start to flap you go up into the air.' Flying is not something which the children accomplish of themselves but something which happens to them, which they suffer. They don't flap their wings, the wings flap them. The dramatic turning from third to second person captures magnificently the significance of this moment.

The pace of the narrative now increases, for all that the extraction of the boots lasts 'all night long'. Only one sentence is given over to the flight — 'it's fun at first but then it gets a bit horrible'. The opening picks up the opening of the previous sentence only to return the tale to its dark course. I was inclined at first to resist the apparent banality of 'a bit horrible', which in this respect reminded me of the earlier phrase 'never stop to say Hello'. But the later phrase is as appropriate in its context as the earlier one. The narrator is reluctant yet to acknowledge the full horror of what is in store, both for the sake of the ending to come and perhaps also for her own sake. Besides, the final act which now begins, though told in a torrent of images and words, is drawn out in time 'all night long'. Bit by bit, indeed, the horror grows.

The rest of the poem is too vivid and too transparent to require commentary. It's worth noting how comprehensively the fall is rendered in terms of sensation — the look back, the sound of the boot as it extricates itself, the feel of the wings coming out. Only the astonishing line of sounds — 'slivery sliding shivering shaking slowly slivering' — holds back the breathless syntax. At the close there is no relief, no gentle release from the story, no waking up in bed, no acknowledgement that after all this is never-never land. 'You can't stop BANG you're dead' and below, two flapping, indifferent boots. Try reading the poem aloud. The ending is remorseless. The audience sits in shock. There's more than a moment's silence.

Moon Wing Boots is both an enactment and a meditation. It treats
of violation and domination, the defining of our humanity by conversation and exchange, purpose and the lack of purpose, reason and
unreason, what it means and does not mean to be a person. I don't
think it's far-fetched to attribute concerns such as these to nine-year-
old writers. If they seem extraordinary that is only the shock of the
ordinary. For narrative, from the start, is a way of defining ourselves
and the world in which we live. An infant's bedtime monologue, a
pre-school child's dictated story, a nine-year-old's poem — these are
all so many attempts, each at its own complex point of development,
incommensurate and unique, to reconstruct the world by way of the
particular forms that constitute narrative thought.

Reconstruction implies both the invention and the discovery of
meaning. It is at this point that it makes sense to confront Carley
Still's Moon Wing Boots with Ted Hughes's Moon Wings. Carley's
poem appropriates its model. She has entered the world of one text
and recreated it in another. The dependence of her poem on the
Hughes poem is too evident to need elaboration but nothing that she
takes from that poem is left as it is, from the moon wings themselves,
reconstituted as boots, to the savage darkening of Hughes's ending.

There is a certain abstraction in Moon Wings, a speculativeness
that never quite comes to life, even in the drawing that faces Hughes's
text. Perhaps if it did come to life the poem would be unreadable to a
class of eight- and nine-year-olds. It takes a nine-year-old herself to
invest these images with demonic energy, turning a poetic fancy into
a nightmare narrative. I will cite just one example of Carley's way
with Hughes — her use of pronouns. I have already mentioned the
sudden eruption of the second person — 'you' — half-way into the
poem and its effect in dramatising the absence of human agency. In
part this effect can be felt in Hughes's poem too and is derived by
Carley from that poem — 'You feel them trying to grow into your
shoulder blades, then they flap and you go'. But Hughes has already
used the second person pronoun. From the outset he has personified
Carley's 'little boys and girls' as 'you'. By witholding the second
person until the very moment of flight Carley brings an urgency to
the imagery which Hughes never attempts. The nightmare which she
builds around Hughes's whiffling wings represents her own particular achievement, her own unique event in the history of the world.
But it's worth remembering that she didn't start from scratch.

Accounts and accountability

In principle I think it is possible to interpret all significant learning as
I have tried to interpret Carley Still's poem, whether the matter in

hand is poetic narrative or scientific experiment, mathematical investigation or interdisciplinary inquiry — the ubiquitous but widely misunderstood primary school 'topic'. Writing in his journal *The Friend* in 1818, the poet Coleridge defined the object of an education of the intellect as being 'to place (the mind) in such relations of circumstance as should gradually excite the germinal power that craves no knowledge but what it can take up into itself, what it can appropriate, and re-produce in fruits of its own'.[3] The learning demonstrated by Carley Still in Moon Wing Boots is of just this kind. I assume that the chief responsibility of a primary school is to create within its classrooms a set of conditions which will stimulate and sustain this style of learning right across the curriculum.

I want to focus attention on those conditions which are implicit within the act of interpretation itself. I have described interpretation as a way of representing to ourselves the learning of our pupils, but it is not enough to represent that learning to ourselves. We have to represent it to our pupils also. We have to make available to them the understanding which we have achieved through interpretation of their present learning in such a way as to incite new learning. Representation is central to accountability.

How do teachers represent to children the quality and potential of their learning? The first requirement is to recognise the authority of children's texts — a term which I intend to refer to learning of many kinds: stories, experiments, investigations inquiries. Not all texts are written. Some are spoken, others drawn, still others enacted. A poem like Moon Wing Boots has an authority that puts our own learning on the spot. It compels us to think again, in this case about the poetry of Ted Hughes among other things. As teachers we are tempted to read such a text chiefly as evidence of its author's present point of development — as a kind of symptom. We treat the poem as marginal. That way we miss its significance, not just as a poem but even as a symptom of development. It is only as we feel challenged by the text that we are in a position to understand at once its accomplishment and its developmental potential.

Let me return to Carley's poem. 'It's fun at first but then it gets a bit horrible.' When I first read the poem I had, as I have explained, a largely negative reaction to these words. It took me some time to understand the use to which Carley had put the apparently trite phrase 'a bit horrible'. I think now that it was only after I had come to appreciate the significance of that earlier and more powerfully naive expression 'never stop to say Hello' that I grew attentive to the nuances of 'bit horrible'. By then the poem had begun to exert its own authority.

It is of critical importance that as Carley's teacher I should represent to her, through conversation and in other ways — and there is no end to a teacher's means in this respect — my understanding of her use of a phrase like this. It does not greatly matter how aware I judge her to have been as to the implications of her particular choice of words. Neither children nor adults are in full control of their material. The limits of interpretation only emerge as the conversation, between reader, writer and text, proceeds. Representation serves a double purpose. By helping to make Carley more conscious of the significance of her chosen language it prepares her, at a later moment in her development as a writer, to seek more elaborate or exact or various or colourful means of achieving her desired effects. That these means are already available to her is evident in her extraordinary evocation of the moment when the boots begin to come out of the children's backs: 'slivery sliding shivering shaking slowly slivering.' The contrast between the complexity of that line and the simplicity of 'It's fun at first but then it gets a bit horrible' is part of the drama of the poem, as it is of Carley herself at this point in time. Later on, if all goes well, a different balance will be struck.

Representation should not be confused with revision, although sometimes the representation to children of the perceived significance of their work may lead them to redraft it. On this occasion I don't think that Carley needs to revise the words 'a bit horrible' and I doubt whether she could, without a sacrifice of poetic authority. Representation looks beyond the immediate moment. It is the means whereby a present achievement is made available for future achievement. Developmentally that is its point.

I have said that the subject of Carley's poem is violation and domination, and, by contrast, the definition of humanity in terms of conversation and exchange. How can I represent to her the grand abstractions which I perceive in her work? I remember reading Moon Wing Boots with Carley beside me. I commented on the ending, asking her if she didn't feel it to be a little too stark. I was still, I suppose, too bound up in the world of Ted Hughes's moon poems to understand Carley's treatment. Her first response was hesitant but in the end she made it clear that she had deliberately rejected Hughes's 'whiffling laugh' in favour of a more savage ending. The nightmare of Carley's imagination, though it appears to discount a happy ending, nevertheless evokes in its magical violence the world of the fairy tale. Fairy tales offer an especially rich opportunity for exploring with children the power of violence and the resistance to violence. (I am thinking not so much of the more remorselessly retold tales as of collections such as Joseph Jacobs' *English Fairy Tales* or Italo Calvino's *Italian Fairy Tales*. The most recent collection of this kind is Angel Carter's *Virago Book of Fairy Tales*, some of which Carley would be fascinated by, though I would need to choose carefully.) They are also, of course, an encyclopaedic repository of narrative techniques. Benjamin again puts it best in 'The Storyteller'. 'The first true storyteller is, and will continue to be, the teller of fairy tales.

Whenever good counsel was at a premium, the fairy tale had it, and where the need was greatest, its aid was nearest. This need was the need created by the myth. The fairy tale tells us of the earliest arrangements that mankind made to shake off the nightmare which the myth had placed upon its chest. In the figure of the fool it shows us how mankind "acts dumb" towards the myth: in the figure of the youngest brother it shows us how one's chances increase as the mythical primitive times are left behind: in the figure of the man who sets out to learn what fear is it shows us that the things we are afraid of can be seen through ... The wisest thing, so the fairy tale taught mankind in olden times, and teaches children to this day, is to meet the forces of the mythical world with cunning and with high spirits.'[4]

In Moon Wing Boots Carley is less optimistic. The mythical world seems irresistible. I cannot foretell how in the end she will herself come to interpret the meaning of the fairy tale, nor do I need to. My task is to direct her towards a literature which might respond to her intellectual concerns as revealed in her poetry and which might equally well provoke further interests in its turn. Carley already enjoys fairy tales, traditional and contemporary. A poem like Moon Wing Boots suggests new tales to read with her and new ways of thinking about them. Other narrative traditions also seem relevant. I was interested to note that in conversation with the class about Carley's poem the story of Perseus was mentioned. We had spent some weeks earlier in the year working on Ancient Greece and its myths and stories. Perhaps the story of Perseus had indeed been an influence on Carley although I suspect that any influence was largely incidental. In any case the mention of Perseus by other children suggests the possibility of returning to an earlier study in the light of a new concern and, at a more general level, of bringing poetry, history and moral thought together in the pursuit of Carley's themes.

It is in ways like this that I try, as a teacher, to represent to children my understanding of their understanding as displayed in a given text. Representation is equally a celebration and an incitement. It makes use of the authority of one text to provoke the next and the next but one. I have examined a single text, but the story of children's learning is not to be found in any one text so much as in the succession of texts over the course of a school career. This succession of texts, which constitutes a kind of intellectual autobiography, defines for me the form which accountability should take in relation to learning. A school's responsibility, as I see it, is to document its pupils' learning from text to text, week by week, term by term and year by year. The most appropriate form which documentation can take is that of the edited archive: a body of work selected, arranged and annotated, by teachers and pupils together, and presented year by year to pupils, as representative of their present accomplishments and indicative of their future learning. The archive is a way of explaining children to themselves. Here they can review the development of their concerns, the onset of new interests, the leaps and setbacks in understanding, the endless search for appropriate forms of expression, the shifting boundaries between constraint and opportunity, the grounding of skill in the succession of significant performances. And because it is the best way of explaining children to themselves it is also the best way of explaining them to their parents and to the world beyond the school. The archive makes learning manifest; no other kind of record can match it.

It is interesting to compare the documentation of children's learning in the form of an archive with the vision of accountability that informs the National Curriculum. The National Curriculum defines attainment in terms of a set of pre-determined targets, arranged in a hierarchical series of levels. Its concerns are with standardisation and with uniformity of performance. Its statements of attainment are predominantly formal in character. They deal with technical accomplishment, irrespective of content. They pay little attention to the significance of children's texts in themselves, that is to say to the meanings which children invent and discover in their most important acts of learning. For me, the most revealing moment in the history of the National Curriculum is the moment at which the members of the English Working Party felt obliged to acknowledge the irrelevance of meaning to its proposed statements of attainment. 'The best writing is vigorous, committed, honest and interesting. We have not included these qualities in our attainment targets because they cannot be mapped onto levels. Even so, all good classroom practice will be geared to encouraging and fostering these vital qualities.'[5] I hope that I am not merely being pessimistic in finding the final sentence too sanguine. Certainly, unless classroom practice is geared to encouraging significant utterance, the teaching of writing, or of any other practice, will fail. The trouble is that by eliminating the significance of children's texts from its measures of attainment the National Curriculum has effectively devalued the texts themselves.

Schools like my own are therefore in something of a quandary. We cannot but acknowledge the demands of the society which we serve, even if the demands, as expressed in Acts of Parliament, are not those of our own pupils or of their parents. At the same time, we cannot but resist these demands. For us, the attainment targets of the National Curriculum have at best a marginal utility. The questions to which we seek answers are idiosyncratic and incommensurable. They focus on children's development as thinkers, with their own individual interests, attitudes, frames of mind and varieties of skill. They revolve around texts, each one of which is unique, for all that they have in common. They are not susceptible to the test. Perhaps in the long run some form of accommodation can be achieved between archive and attainment level, interpretation and quantification. At present we simply don't know.

For the most part I have been concerned in this paper with one child's text and with accountability to the individual learner. But in the classroom, accountability often takes a more collaborative form. Children share their texts with each other as well as with their teachers and a teacher's representations are often informed by the common experience of the class. Moreover, in giving to parents an account of children's learning, the collective activity of the classroom is as significant as an individual pupil's texts. The walls of a lively classroom sparkle with the work of the class. Learning in the primary school has a very public face.

When I think back over last year at my own school one particular event comes to mind which articulates our vision of education. A young Polish artist visited the school to run a workshop on the art of paper cutting with children from our own school and from the four other village schools in our neighbourhood. After the stimulation of the workshop, the children returned to their own schools and classes and each class spent a month using the technique of paper cutting to explore aspects of the life of its own village, past and present. During this period of investigation the artist visited each school in turn, helping children to exploit their various ideas in the chosen medium of expression. At the end of the month an exhibition of the finished work was mounted at the local museum and parents and friends were invited to view it. The inexhaustible variety of the children's responses to the challenge of their project was there for all to see, scattered about the Renaissance splendour of the old Abingdon Town Hall. It was, as Jola Scicinska put it, 'a celebration of people and their surroundings', significant both in itself and also, however distantly, 'as one of the necessary steps to end all oppression'. A good deal, perhaps the greater part, of school learning falls short of this condition. But this, or something like it, is our aim. In the end it is to this that we are held accountable.

References

1   Hughes, T. *Moon Whales*, Faber and Faber, 1988.
2   Benjamin, W. 'The Storyteller', in Arendt, H. (ed.) *Illuminations*, Harcourt Brace and Ward, 1968.
3   *Collected Works of Samuel Taylor Coleridge*, Vol 4, Routledge and Kegan Paul, 1969.
4   Benjamin, op cit.
5   *English for Ages 5 to 11* HMSO, 1988.

3.2 The truth that is within us

Christine Webb

It is a Thursday in March. It might be any Thursday; it might be the day after I had agreed to write this paper. The idea of accountability and how we cope with it is growing in my mind, nourishing itself on the events of the day.

Let me give the day a context. Thursday is a full teaching day, with no non-contact time; it is also the day when I am responsible for the duty team at breaks. As a result I am by definition late all day: theoretically I should be out in the corridors and playground areas the instant the end-of-lesson bell rings, while simultaneously seeing my own class out of the room; and back in the classroom ready to receive the next class at the end of breaks while still hustling pupils into the building and causing them to pick up litter en route. It is impossible to describe this experience without sounding like Joyce Grenfell's nursery teacher (and frequently impossible to do it without turning into her) — and yet it is the stuff of which daily life in school is made.

Today I plan as I drive to school. I have come to a critical point with two of my classes, a Year 10 and a Year 11 GCSE group. I have decided how I want to proceed, but have not prepared the materials. This is largely because I have spent the previous weekend and the evenings of this week finishing my A level 'mock' marking, and although I feel triumphant at finishing on time, I am anxious about today's lessons. Already, in fact, the rival accountabilities of the day are asserting themselves: the duty to one's current exam classes in terms of preparation and practice for external papers has taken precedence over the duty of detailed lesson planning — yet the lessons involved are also the exam classes, and the work is likely to form part of their final assessment. It is as always necessary to live on one's wits. I enjoy doing this, if I am honest, but the necessity is sometimes wearing.

I arrive in school early and go to the faculty office, where I use the BBC computer to type out a list of assignments. The office is cramped and untidy, and I wonder desultorily whether any of us is likely to have time to do a blitz on it. I was intending to do this myself a few days ago, but someone came along with a problem or an idea to discuss, and we did that instead. My gospel is 'people before things', but I tend to forget that if I lose sight of — or simply lose — the things, the people suffer.

In the staffroom working area I run off copies of my typed sheet, and see various members of the faculty. As always I am struck by their energy and versatility: one is about to launch a new after-school club, one has recently taken on fresh responsibilities as a librarian, one has invited my comments at a Year 7 oral assessment of much ingenuity and success, one has taught a first A level course with great gusto. Yet these are all people whose lives have been touched by private stress — death, divorce, a new baby, the demands of changing family life. At times they look worn with anxiety or grief. Somehow they rise to the demand of each minute, and today with the idea of this paper in my mind I ask myself afresh, How do they do it?

In the corridor, on the way to registration, the answer presents itself in bodily form. Groups of children and adolescents dawdle, scurry or hurl themselves towards the classrooms; some are immersed in intent conversation, some are shrieking with laughter, scorn or rage, some greet their teachers with the ebullient 'Hello Miss — Hello Sir' which they will repeat though they meet you 20 times a day. A few are turned inward, shrinking into themselves with fear or anger; the word 'problem' precedes them like a red flag. It is not, I remind myself, that we love all the children we meet: simply, they are there. They are there as I open the classroom door for the short tutorial session. I could take the register without glancing at it if need were: this is our fourth year together as a tutor group and we know each other well. I look round to see if the persistent latecomers and malingerers are here yet (a note to the Education Welfare Officer about Jenny F. perhaps?) and also to gauge the emotional temperature. A small group is in huddled conversation, shoulders angled to keep everybody out; another more relaxed group is brandishing with shrieks of disbelief some photographs just unearthed of themselves at 12 years old. In this time, which to me seems like the twinkling of an eye, they feel they have experienced a universe of change. I beckon to one of them and enquire about yesterday's absence. A curiously constrained look crosses her face, and I can see that she is also judging how much to reveal.

'Miss, do you remember?' — and she names an ex-pupil of her own age, transferred two years ago.

'M'm?'

'Well — don't tell anyone, Miss, will you, but she had a baby and it died. And me and some others, we went to the funeral yesterday.'

'It died? How old was it?'

'Well, Miss, it lived about five minutes, I think. But don't tell none of the other teachers, will you?'

I am used to not expressing shock, but I find I have shut my eyes for an instant at the image of this immature mother and her dead baby. I send my informant back to her friends and open the register.

The usual scatter of messages falls out — a meeting about the skiing trip, a late library-book reminder, a note from the school office about a discrepancy in my register return last week. I put the arithmetical mistake right, and push to the back of my mind for the moment the question of whether anyone else should be told about the ex-pupil's baby. But I have been asked not to tell. The bell goes for first lesson.

I enjoy the first lesson with my group of mainstream 15-year-olds, to whom I give out my duplicated sheet. One of the assignments involves dreams, which we discuss animatedly — some unexpected contributors join in, as I had hoped — and eventually all settle to work on chosen assignments. I impose a period of absolute silence and self-supporting work during this lesson, simply so that I can complete some preparation for the next one. We are all wholly absorbed for the time it takes me to write out my next set of ideas for *The Merchant of Venice*, and at the end of 20 minutes almost everyone is eager to consult. There are still cries of 'Just read this through, Miss' as we're packing up, but I deal rather hastily with the last one and make for the corridor. Passing the lavatories I put my head round the door (holding my breath) and check that all is well; then I take my *Merchant of Venice* topics, set the photocopier to run off 30 sheets and pick up a cup of tea. Back in the corridor I do a quick circuit, trying to spot all my duty team; two or three are not well, and I feel a vague guilt at having to remind one of them.

Now for Year 11. This class of 30, in the last full term of the GCSE course, is one of my delights. I have taught them for three years, and shall miss them when they go. Today for part of the time I am team-teaching: a colleague takes the majority of the class while I assess a small-group discussion separately. This group has chosen to discuss religious attitudes and beliefs, and I listen and watch with interest as Sikh, Christian and agnostic ideas are exchanged. The high point for me comes when someone says 'No — I really want to hear what you think'.

Back in the classroom my colleague and I circulate among the pupils as they argue and scribble their way towards an understanding of Portia. At one point the two teachers engage in a spirited argument about Portia's integrity; the class enjoys this clash of opinion, and we both play up accordingly. In this year-group we have chosen, as a faculty, to have five larger English classes instead of six smaller ones, and to use our sixth teacher for team-teaching: we have all profited from this, and it has been very enjoyable. I reflect mournfully that it will not be possible in future because of the constraints of the timetable. Is it worth fighting to alter this? No, because I know I cannot win: our timetable gets more nearly impossible every year, and our timetablers have always squeezed miracles of accommodation out of it. Keep your energy for battles that are worth fighting.

During the lunch-hour an educational publisher sets up a display in the staffroom. Most of the faculty gathers around, and our Second in Faculty reminds us about the capitation money in hand. Two orders have proved to be out of print and we have a couple of hundred pounds left — which we shall lose if we don't spend before the end of term. Our stock for Year 8 is shabby and old-fashioned, and several items on display seem sharply appropriate. I make a snap decision and spend £250 at a stroke, and worry about it for several days. In fact the books when they arrive are a great success with the children (something I find impossible to predict even after all these years); but I have added up incorrectly and overspent by £100. At the very end of March, however, yet another previous order is revealed to be out of print, and the one bill cancels out the other.

It is the afternoon. Time to give the A level students their 'mock' papers back. They have done unexpectedly well, and I almost hesitate to tell them so, since it is so ingrained in me that the 'mocks' are always a disaster. We look together at the papers, I point out one obvious aspect of a question which I had not noticed but they had all identified, and they all preen themselves. C has done better than he really deserves, and J is depressed by his poor marks; S gives a shriek of delight at her grade, and F speaks for the first time in weeks. I look at them fondly, and pray that we can keep up the impetus until June.

After break (more break duty, more lavatories) I have an hour and 10 minutes with a lower-ability Year 9 group. There are eight of these left, gradually being transferred to mainstream groups; all are due to go by Easter. One of them is never absent, but we can perm any five of the other seven; continuity is therefore difficult, and at the end of Thursday they are always tired and usually cross. At present we are slowly working our way through 'My Life and Times', and the toll of writing is judiciously interspersed with photographs, plans and family trees. At the start of the project everyone plotted a 'memory web', a simple diagram outline of possible categories of memory, and several of them constantly return to this to make new and ever more decorative versions of it. As constantly, I intercept these attempts and urge them slowly on to write 'just five more sentences'.

The patterns of English words still enmesh them in a desperate maze where they wander blankly: 'Miss, how do you spell . . .?' I give them a hint, and direct them to the dictionary.

'Oh, Miss, can't you just tell me?'

'No, the dictionary is your FRIEND.'

At this, they make horrible faces. Earlier, I have read them the passage from *Cider with Rosie* where Spadge Hopkins lifts up the teacher and puts her on top of the cupboard, before leaving the school *for ever*. They roared with delight, but looked envious. Fortunately there are no high cupboards in the room.

As half past three approaches we make individual homework contracts. They record these laboriously, with expressions of unmelting virtue, but as the bell rings and they are released into private life, I can hear them making such joyful plans for the evening as will sabotage their homework completely.

There is a pause in the momentum of the day at this point, and I will take advantage of it to introduce a diagram of my own. This is the formal and legal context of the day — the map of accountabilities. It is not normally prominent in my mind, nor I think in any teacher's, and it is only when priorities come into conflict that most of us give a thought to it. The practical demands create so complex a daily texture as to absorb one's attention — though those too can conflict, as they have done today. This first diagram (Figure 1) is the formal one. Its

Figure 1   Formal lines of responsibilities

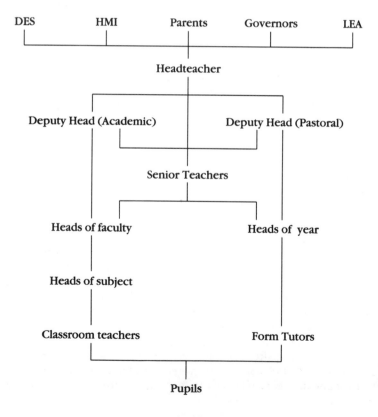

direction seems to suggest an upward flow of accountabilities: the bodies at the top, whether professionally qualified or personally involved, require account to be given by the whole of the structure below. A teacher on the base line must follow a scheme of work, prepare lessons, organise and run the classroom, mark, assess, and evaluate and in these and many other ways must satisfy the head of subject (let us say of history) who is responsible for the teaching of the subject and who will in turn be part of a larger grouping of subjects within a faculty (in this case humanities). The head of humanities (who will also be the head of one of the individual subjects — geography, history, RE, economics, sociology — within the faculty) must run and negotiate the faculty budget, maintain a unified faculty policy in terms of classroom approaches, teaching methods and style and be responsible both for schemes of work and for the assessment, recording and reporting of the work of pupils (an element which becomes larger and very much more complex with the development of the National Curriculum). The final examination results of pupils are also the responsibility of the faculty head, who must evaluate and (where necessary) seek to improve them: these are the yardstick by which the school will be judged by all those bodies at the head of the chart — and by which colleagues judge each other.

On the other side of the chart the line of accountability runs upward from the form tutor who has pastoral responsibility for a group of pupils (usually of the same age) to a head of year who organises and oversees the work of a team of tutors. Some of the work is formal and administrative — registration, absences, sending information home; some is pastoral or disciplinary — dealing with behaviour problems and, more time-consuming and less easily defined, their causes; a great deal, both for the form tutor and the head of year, is about the delicate and complex business of personal relationships.

Different schools have different ways of managing and delegating areas of responsibility, depending on the strengths of individuals. Some staff at senior teacher level may have responsibilities on the academic side, such as that of examinations secretary — a role involving constant communication and correspondence, as well as requiring powerful administrative ability; some may be involved on the pastoral side, for example in charge of careers, liaising with a multitude of outside bodies as well as counselling at some stage every pupil in the school; one senior teacher is likely at present to be the finance officer, struggling to stretch a newly delegated budget, like strudel pastry over a vast surface. Beyond these figures stand — or stagger — those of the deputy heads, who may be constructing a timetable, dealing with child abuse, mediating to achieve peace and compromise out of a confrontation, receiving the queries, anxieties and complaints of staff . . . and teaching. And the headteacher? As has been well said in another paper in this collection, the head is an embodier. At once symbol and target, the head represents the school to the outside world, and to itself. The head presents the school to the governors, and the governors to the school — a much more important process, and an infinitely trickier one, than it used to be. The head gives the bad news — about cuts, about inspections, about how long it will take to get the roof fixed. The head listens to violent children, desperate parents, fraught teachers; to politicians and the local press; to the ambitious, the triumphant and the mortally sick. The job never stops. I can't imagine how they get people to do it.

The classroom teacher, of course, meets these various levels of the structure directly, as well as through the medium of others in the structure. One may at different times of the day and the week be talking to a parent, a visiting governor, an HMI or local inspector, as well as to the head and one's colleagues; but these encounters, however important, make up only so many minor threads in a pattern whose texture is the constant encounter with the pupils. The children, as I said near the start of this paper, are always there. So I would add to the flow-chart of accountabilities some elements which were missing in the first version (see Figure 2).

Figure 2   Some additional relationships

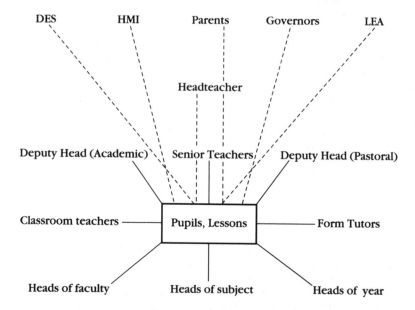

Altering the emphasis of the chart like this makes it into something different — not a flow-chart at all. Now the pupils are at the heart of it; and indeed when I sketched out a first tentative map for myself 'pupils' was the category I put in first. They are the most compelling element in the daily routine, and infinitely the most important. From 'pupils' I moved to 'parents': they are more likely to ask for the account to be rendered than are the pupils and, as we know, they have a legal right to it; teachers are aware, too, of dealing with parents through pupils as well as directly. Parents are, most importantly, the major part of the pupil's context, the world which supports or fails or even destroys the child. Teachers who are mothers or fathers have their own daily experience of this truth; we can all draw on our own history as children to remind us.

But much closer to teachers in the course of the day's work than parents is the subject-matter of their lessons. In my experience teachers can be divided into two broad groups in this matter. Some can teach virtually anything — given a reasonable chance to prepare it and, obviously, not too senior or specialist a level to reach — and these are often the most gifted, for their gift is the gift of pedagogy itself. They have a natural rapport with the young, they can adapt themselves apparently effortlessly to a class of any size, age or level and they can draw, again it seems instinctively, on a wide range of techniques of communication. The other group may well also have these gifts, but their abiding passion is the subject that they teach. They communicate with their pupils through the power of this enthusiasm and the passionate belief that it is important. In one department where I worked we had a saying: 'All think that their subject is the most important, but OURS REALLY IS'.

Without one of these sustaining forces it is, I think, well-nigh impossible to remain a classroom teacher. Sometimes one is bursting with a fresh insight about one's subject which it is vital to pass on to some group of pupils; sometimes the focus of a day is the development of personalities and abilities, the slow acquisition of a skill, the establishing and maintaining of a working relationship. But when there is satisfaction to be found neither in the subject nor in the relationship with the pupils — when the classroom becomes a battleground or a desert — then darkness falls. We suffer then that humiliation which D.H. Lawrence saw as the daily experience of teaching, and trudge onwards for days, or weeks, or months, hoping that the darkness will lift. It happens to almost everyone at one time or another; most teachers will recognise what I describe.

At time like this it is the part of colleagues to support the teacher. Looking back at the diagram it seems to me that the network of relationships operates in another way than the official. Individual teachers are responsible to their faculties, their faculty members and heads, and to their colleagues in the school's pastoral structure, in the ways that I have described, and these lines of the network lead up to the deputy heads and to the head. But individual colleagues within faculty and pastoral structures, and less formally in the daily interchange of the staffroom, are responsible for the welfare of each other. We could all make a private network, in some ways more important than this formal one, of the colleagues to whom people turn in need; and we could equally easily think of schools in which we have taught where some element of the structure — and that means some person — was so weak as to disable the teacher at the precise point where help was most needed. No structure in itself, however well designed, can compensate for the tyrannical or capricious headteacher, the incompetent faculty head or the malicious staffroom gossip. Blessed are they who work in a school where teachers care for one another, for they shall survive.

While pupil contact forms the minute-by-minute reality of teaching one's subject, and discussion with colleagues both its measure and its support, its boundaries are formally defined by syllabus, examination boards and the National Curriculum. The revision of that syllabus, the new demands of the examination boards and, most alarmingly present in many teachers' minds, the arrival of the National Curriculum, have changed the life of the classroom teacher radically in the course of the last five or six years. These years correspond, as it happens, to the years of my own appointment in my current school. When I arrived we were planning the work and teaching of the new GCSE courses, while simultaneously finishing the last year of O level and CSE; there was a lot of concern about the implications of a single course for all, about the choice of balance between coursework and examination, about the massive responsibilities of assessing and moderating all our pupils' work. Above all, there was the constant current of anxiety — which runs like the daily flow of time itself through every teacher's consciousness — that every new development was being tried out in practice and modified as we went along. We had to remind ourselves that neither we, our knowledge and expertise, nor the nature of the children had changed overnight; and that indeed much of what GCSE brought with it was exactly what we had long hoped for, what many had worked for and what some had fought for. How well I remember those sessions with our department (we were not called a faculty then) in which we reviewed, planned and reassured! At the end of the first year, and even more at the end of the second when the first GCSE year group were awarded their grades, we were jubilant. We had enjoyed the fresh emphasis of the work, our pupils really had developed skills both traditional and new — and our judgement had been upheld: the results were sound. No matter (we felt) that we had carried out our enormous assessment task under intense pressure of time, and unpaid; the reward was in terms of seeing our professionalism vindicated — in the eyes of pupils, parents, governors, even (it seemed for a brief, heady time) in the eyes of the nation. It could be seen that we knew what we were doing; we had rendered our account.

But the account, it appears, has not been accepted.

> Everyman, where art thou going
> So gaily? Hast thou thy maker forgot?

In the medieval play, it is when Everyman is at his most joyously confident that the summons comes. He is to present his book of account that very day, and does not know how to begin. Had we been as irresponsible as Everyman, we might not now be feeling so bitter at the demand of the angel of death (I refer of course to the National Curriculum, rather than to any particular Minister); but this demand is not so much for the book of account as for a re-writing of it in ingeniously devised columnar form, according to a revised method of celestial or diabolical calculation. Whatever else I may say in this paper about the maintaining of confidence, to very many teachers it seems as if the aim of recent successive administrations has been to degrade, de-motivate and denounce them. Many primary teachers have spoken privately and have — bravely — written publicly about the assessment methods and their implications in terms of resources, time and results; many seem appalled equally by the mountainous labour involved and by the diminutive mouse of genuinely new information produced. Secondary teachers, already engaged in moderation and its accompanying administration, watch the approach of this tide of work with something like horror. Already, for example, science departments which have energetically revised their whole lower school teaching schemes in the light of the National Curriculum have seen their work nullified by a drastic change in the requirements. Similar shifts are at work in the teaching of history. These are not, then, simply times of change, but times of desperation, almost of persecution. Like the protagonist of a folk-tale, we face tasks that by definition are impossible, yet in which failure carries unthinkable implications: where then shall we find the necessary heroic strength?

Many of the other formal and enforcing bodies plotted in my diagram — the school's governing body, the LEA, the local inspectorate or advisory team, HMI, DES — have also, during the period of which I write, undergone a radical change in their composition, duties, powers or mode of operation; some of these changes have been equally profound in their effect of the teacher. I have watched teachers of all ages and at all stages of their careers adapting themselves to these changes with, as might be expected, ritual grumbles; with private reservations and sometimes deep personal anxiety; but above all with amazing flexibility and with some central value that makes them temper their often justifiable outrage at extra burdens placed upon them with an almost blameable moderation. What is that central value? Can we find in it our heroic strength? And will that strength be, as it has always been, to enable us to continue, or shall we at some point have to say 'enough'?

These questions are not in the forefront of my mind, but they are not entirely absent from it, on the Thursday with which this account begins, as I walk down the corridor at something after three-thirty. I make a call to the curriculum support teacher (money again, this time about 'Inset' time for National Curriculum training), and write a note to a colleague in the school with which we share a campus, about some sixth-form teaching, also shared by both schools. Then I heat a meal in the microwave which two never-to-be-forgotten colleagues have given to the staffroom on their retirement last year, and eat it while talking to an independent financial adviser who has called to see if any staff are interested in insurance or investment. Fantasising about early-early retirement I burn myself on the pasta, and swear inelegantly, something I try not to do in school. Then it is five o'clock, and the Year 11 parents' consultation is about to begin. Half-heartedly, I take some marking along to my classroom, in case there are gaps between the appointments. But there are none, and I am immersed all evening in brief intense conversations. I value and often enjoy these meetings — there are always moments of illumination and communication, often not where I had expected them — but I am also aware of that undertow of anxiety running in the dark bottom of the stream. What if tonight is the night which will reveal to all my private weaknesses, my fallings-short and my simple inadequacy for the huge task of my profession? But none of this happens. We discuss the technical problems of one pupil, the hopes for further education of another, the perfectionism of a third. Mostly, the parents and I discuss all this with the pupil, for the majority of my Year 11 class have accepted the challenge to attend the meeting themselves. 'She only wants to HUMILIATE us' drawled a cynic earlier this week, and we could all laugh at the picture I drew of possible embarrassments for us all, including me. The potential embarrassment is there, all the same, and I mentally salute my pupils for confronting it.

It is well after nine o'clock, and I have over-run. I get into the car, grateful that tomorrow is Friday and a light day. I do not reflect at all on the way home, but just experience the privacy, absorbing thankfully the darkness of streets and fields in the early spring night. Only next day do I look back and jot down a list of the events of Thursday, since it already seems to me to have touched upon many of the diverse aspects of teaching and, perhaps, shown some of the sources from which the demands for accountability come.

The briefest encounter of the day was probably the call to the curriculum support teacher; but that call made a link through her to the LEA (though that link is already changing as we take on the management of our own budget); and it also represented the link with the DES, since the 'Inset' money was allocated to us in respect of the National Curriculum. So, though brief, that exchange was probably the one with the most power to shape the days and lessons of all the pupils and teachers for whom I am responsible. Contacts with colleagues about books, money, teaching and non-teaching duties and (not least) personal matters had nodded in the direction of other areas of accountability — maintaining the faculty resources, balancing (just) the books, simply noticing that everything was running — as well as keeping up that contact with adults which helps teachers to stay sane. I had also given personal accounts to quite a number of parents of what I thought I was up to with my Year 11 class.

In all this I find I am not much nearer to identifying for others or even finding for myself a source of heroic strength. Such strength as we have I think comes very substantially from each other, from the support which teams of people can create. Another source lies in sheer physical stamina: outsiders often comment that 'you must be very patient' to be a teacher; but I am not at all a patient person, and think the main requirement of the job is inexhaustible energy. At the heart, however, there must be some sort of self-esteem. There is a lovely story of a bright young adviser visiting a school and enquiring of the tough, wiry deputy head, 'Who do you hold yourself accountable to?' She fixes him with her glittering eye, and replies, 'The children, and God'. Some of us will have to replace God in that answer with a more fallible authority, but the equation is essentially the same: honest endeavour towards the pupils plus honest transmission of the truth that is within you equals (you hope) enough peace of mind to sleep in your bed at night. At any rate, those are the standards to which we all turn when priorities seriously clash. No legal framework, no formal map, no economically viable flow chart can support you if you feel you are failing in those central truths.

I will end on a lighter note. In my very first year of teaching, over a quarter of a century ago, I was lucky enough to read an article deploring the emphasis on dedication as a necessary qualification for teachers. It was a sane, witty article — it was, of course, in *The Guardian* — and I can still remember large parts of it. At the end, the writer observed: 'Teaching is a job, like any other. At the end of the month they give you money for doing it, and no one has ever been known not to take it.'

3.3 Individuals in partnership

Jaki Stewart

It is reassuring to remember that my ultimate responsibility is to individual children for their education during their time at our co-educational day school for primary children with emotional and behavioural difficulties. It is reassuring, for despite current uncertainties and the variety and complexity of the teacher's accountabilities, the children remain paramount and their company a pleasure. I respect young people and this underpins my practice and stimulates my endeavour to 'get it right'. I am accountable to each child for education in that an account is rendered to individuals of the purpose and approach of all activities, the 'whys' of 'what and how we are doing things'. Learning experiences are frequently evaluated, formally and informally together, both in the short and longer term.

However, whilst this centrality of the child is the essence of teaching, to maximise the opportunities for the child's education my accountability as a teacher must acknowledge the child's parents (or guardians) as the so-called 'consumers'; the governors of the school as the local 'decision-makers'; the government as legislators; the LEA as my present contractual employers, and the headteacher as my immediate 'line manager'.

Recent government reforms concerning the powers of governing bodies, local management and the proposed 'parents' charter' prompt us to start mapping out the future for our accountability. Following from the clarification of the main parties to whom I am accountable, centring around the child, a discussion of the nature of my responsibility to them is required.

Personally, I am responsible for my own pedagogy (including certain aspects of my choice of teaching and learning styles) and my understanding and familiarity with the extent and nature of each child's emotional, behavioural and attendant learning difficulties, and my knowledge of good practice.

I am accountable to, and share responsibility with, my co-teacher for planning, implementing and evaluating the curriculum for the individuals in our class, which obviously requires our joint responsibility to keep updated methods of assessment, monitoring and recording of individual pupils' progress. The school's, LEA's and central government's policies have to be honoured, and my co-teacher and I are accountable to them for this.

Our class team also includes two dedicated classroom assistants, and my co-teacher and I are responsible for ensuring that we do indeed work as a team, and enable them to undertake their roles as classroom assistants effectively within our team.

In the wider context of the whole school, as a teacher I am co-ordinator of the 'scientific' and 'personal and social education' (PSE) aspects of the curriculum. The post of a curriculum co-ordinator involves a range of special responsibilities: with PSE we are trying to establish a whole-school approach which highlights the active promotion of all children's (and staff's) self-esteem and a caring ethos. I am responsible for my own contribution to this ethos in all my interactions with children and staff during my day at school and as part of the whole-school team.

It has been established legally for many years that the duty of education rests ultimately with parents. A teacher's accountability to parents includes helping them to fulfil their obligations for their child's education, to ensure that the system responds appropriately. This requires the teacher to offer comprehensive information and explanation and actively to receive information in turn. Accepting insights from their unique experience of the child enables parents to be regarded as partners with professionals in helping their children, a concept which was stressed in the Warnock Report (1978).[1] A true dialogue is formed, which when appropriate also involves the child.

Teachers need to recognise the parent as a very powerful educator and to communicate their own professionalism, including the characteristics of 'good practice' and the criteria on which judgements are made. To this end, some schools hold pre-year meetings for groups of parents during which teachers explain their approaches to teaching and learning and discuss these with parents.

Termly parents' evenings at our school concentrate on the individual child, reviewing progress from our two perspectives (or ideally three, if the child is able to participate) and discussing the aims and approaches to be best adopted in the different curricular areas with regard to the child's 'special needs'. These discussions are 'logged' and signed as a record of the conversation by both teacher and parent, and provide a starting point for evaluation at the following meeting.

When it is appropriate and feasible, parents become involved in the child's learning in the classroom. Such involvement requires thorough planning and organisation, but it recognises the value of parents in school.

Parents are urged to contact school with concerns or information they feel it would be beneficial for us to know, at any time — just as we contact them on a similar basis. Unlike a local mainstream school, we miss the daily contact with parents in the playground as our children are 'bussed' to school. We use the telephone, home-school books, post and, if necessary, home visits to share information about both positive and negative behaviour and learning.

For some children difficult home circumstances certainly exacerbate their problems. For them it is of even greater importance that we attempt to develop a 'partnership' with their parents — initially perhaps by visiting them at home if they are unable or unwilling to visit school, or by involving other agencies, like the educational social worker.

We create opportunities to meet in different contexts. Social events like barbecues and regular coffee mornings are organised, with transport provided if necessary. Parents are invited to share our displays of learning at the Christmas production, book week and sports day, and are kept up-to-date through the school newsletter of happenings at school. We raise funds together (which have recently contributed to the installation of a soft play room) and all events are publicised by the excitement and enthusiasm of the children, as well as the more formal 'letter home'.

Thus, as SEAC (1990) stated: 'written reports are only part of the reporting relationship.' Developing this, Records of Achievement are becoming the means of reporting annually to parents. Parents are increasingly 'eager to participate in, and respond to their child's record',[2] creating a partnership in which all parties (including the child) are exercising their accountabilities.

As parents share in the partnership with teachers, their participation in the decision-making becomes more evident. They show genuine interest in the affairs of the school as affecting their child, based on their thorough understanding of the current situation and their feeling of 'being part of it'.

A similar partnership is created with governors. With so many of them inexperienced and facing increased powers, the teachers' accountability to them is initially to enable them to make decisions. In so doing our accountability to them is similar to that of our responsibility to parents: to re-consider our 'openness' and provide more information about what goes on.

Greater knowledge of the teachers' practice and roles will also make the profession less vulnerable and will form the foundation of the trusting partnership between governors, parents and the school — with the child at its heart.

The exercise of the teachers' and governors' accountabilities in establishing their partnership is time consuming — just as activities with parents take time. We try to build a relationship which starts by governors' visiting the school as regularly as possible (problematic if they are in full-time employment) and becoming familiar with the children, the staff, the ethos we create together and our approaches to learning. Governors come in to lunch with us (staff and children), and we welcome their presence in the classroom as often as possible, in addition to the more usual invitations to productions and other events involving the children. Here they also meet parents, as they do in the more social contexts we arrange.

Staff and governors socialise before governors' meetings. However staff are frequently involved in the 'formal' meetings themselves — perhaps by presenting a draft policy for discussion or raising each other's awareness about different issues.

I turn now to my own practice in school, which I regard as fulfilling my contractual accountabilities to my present employer, the LEA, overseen by my 'line manager', the headteacher.

My personal responsibility to create conductive 'conditions of learning'[3] by way of my qualities, skills and knowledge of good practice, particularly with regard to classroom management, has had to change little with recent legislation. The LEA defines the curriculum as consisting of 'all the activities which are planned or encouraged within each school to promote the intellectual, personal, social, emotional and physical development of its pupils. It includes not only the formal programme as described by schemes of work and the timetable; but also the style and management of the school; the many features which combine to produce the school's ethos; the attention to cross-curricular issues; and the teaching and learning styles which are adopted'.[4]

I am accountable to and share responsibility with my co-teacher for planning and implementing this in class, and it is our joint responsibility to take into account the school's, authority's and government's policies, and to keep updated our methods of assessment, monitoring and recording of individual pupils' progress.

It is only relatively recently that 'education in the ordinary sense, not therapy and treatment, is now taken for granted'[5] for children with emotional and behavioural difficulties. It was the Warnock Report[6] which justified such 'education' for all pupils formally for the first time.

According to the National Curriculum Council 'the principle that all pupils should now receive a broad and balanced curriculum, relevant to their individual needs, is now for the first time established in law. For pupils with special educational needs this entitlement represents an opportunity to improve standards further, building on the advances of recent years as highlighted in the Warnock Report (1978) and the 1981 Act'.[7]

The LEA suggests that the nine areas of experience identified by HMI (aesthetic and creative, human and social, linguistic and literary, mathematical, moral, physical, scientific, spiritual and technological) should be used as a way of planning and analysing the curriculum for breadth and balance. With regard to pupil entitlement, the 5-16 curriculum policy states: 'All pupils should be taught Religious Education and the core and other foundation subjects of the National Curriculum. Schools should also ensure that cross-curricular themes are introduced or developed in a manner appropriate to the age and needs of the pupils.' It is also recommended that opportunities should be provided for 'pupils at different stages to follow appropriate courses of study in a range of other subjects'.[8]

Thus, 'the National Curriculum is not synonymous with the "whole" curriculum. Neither do statutory orders for the core and foundation subjects set out how the attainment targets should be taught'.[9] For most children in our school, access can be provided to the curriculum and particularly the core subjects (English, mathematics and science) by paying careful attention to the quality of certain foundation areas and cross-curricular themes, and by differentiation of curriculum and learning strategies to accord with specific needs identified by the school and in statements of special educational needs.

Assessment of pupil progress is by observation and analysis of the individual's recording and practical work as well as other forms of assessment, like reading and number tests, and the imminent Standard Assessment Tasks. The keeping of records devised by curriculum co-ordinators supports such assessments and they are updated when appropriate.

The LEA policy states that the assessment of pupils' performance and progress 'should identify individual pupils' strengths and weaknesses, contribute to planning the next steps in their learning, and lead to further diagnostic assessment where necessary; it should involve them in discussion of their work and in self-appraisal; and it should inform the pupils, parents and others of their progress and performance'.[10] To this end, the LEA 'Record of Achievement' is becoming the 'vehicle for the assessment requirements of the National Curriculum, the means of reporting annually to parents and the umbrella under which achievement within, across and beyond the curriculum can be celebrated and recorded'.[11]

The Record of Achievement contains a summary document and a pupil portfolio. The summary document is an ongoing process and contains information on the school and a personal statement by the pupil referring to achievements, experiences and interests. There is also 'a broad and positive summary of the student's achievement and experiences, encompassing the whole curriculum, out-of-school activities, personal attributes and skills and the most recent National Curriculum assessments' in the form of a curriculum statement within the summary document.[12]

The pupil portfolio contains a selection by the pupil of work about which they are particularly proud, and which illustrates a range of curricular experiences. 'Pupil portfolio is a means of laying the foundations for self-knowledge and the skills of self-expression.'[13] Particularly in a school environment such as ours, the dialogue created between teacher and child with regard to the portfolio promotes self-confidence and recognises 'achievement across the breadth of their experiences both in and out of school'.[14]

There is presently much anxiety and concern about testing and assessment. I find it reassuring to remind myself that, as my accountability is to the child, so assessment is intrinsic to the curriculum (planning and implementation), teaching/learning and evaluation. Its function understood, my efforts will concentrate upon the consolidation of the assessment framework so that it meets the needs of all pupils and the different areas of the curriculum.

My individual and shared teaching responsibilities occur within a class team which includes two classroom assistants. An extension of my accountability is ensuring that we do all work together. An understanding of the classroom assistants' role is fundamental. They give care (physical and emotional) and support (learning and emotional development) for the child and they support the teacher, particularly in: classroom organisation; through moral support; and by becoming involved in the learning and observation of individual children.

It is important too that the classroom assistants understand the teacher's role. The fostering of teamwork involves team members in identifying their own and each others' talents so that tasks can be delegated appropriately and individuals develop their potential. We accept the responsibility to take initiatives and make the decisions. Our intentions and expectations of individuals' learning (academic and behaviour) require clear and positive expression, orally and in writing.

All team members have such knowledge of the purpose of each activity for each child or group of children (planning meetings being vital in this respect) and can comment on the relative success of each activity for each individual, thus providing a record of the child's progress.

At the end of each school day there is an evaluative team meeting in which such assessments are expanded upon and individuals about whom we are most concerned, discussed.

As a member of the team of teachers throughout the school, communication is as important as it is within a class. Twice a week all teachers meet for discussion and in-service training.

I am leader of the 'science' and 'PSE' curriculum 'areas' and as such it is my responsibility in consultation with the headteacher, other staff and governors, to formulate school policies and to co-ordinate curriculum development in these areas.

Curriculum development has drawn on my curriculum skills (including subject knowledge and professional judgement) and inter-personal skills (concerning working with colleagues and external representation). I am required to monitor the implementation of the science and PSE policies throughout the school and, in consultation with the other teachers, develop appropriate procedures for assessment and record keeping. This, together with the identification of other needs, has required my organisation of school-based in-service training sessions and workshops.

I have enjoyed supporting colleagues in their own classrooms, and where possible I have tried to use my own classroom situation as an example in the organisation and practice of science and PSE.

To keep abreast of the latest developments and new resources I attend the appropriate courses and co-ordinators' meetings, and I find it helpful to liaise with support teachers and other schools.

The ordering and organisation of equipment and resources in consultation with the headteacher is another aspect of my curricular responsibility.

'Policy-making' and a 'planned curriculum' are certainly two key elements in a school's approach to PSE, but 'the commitment of everyone to work towards establishing a healthy environment and ethos, in which individuals are valued and respected and positive relationships fostered, will provide a sound basis for personal and social education'.[15]

As a member of the whole-school team, I am responsible for my contribution to its caring ethos in all I do. My pedagogy and the ways in which I approach the curriculum, assessment and work as a team member and curriculum co-ordinator affect and will be reflected through the school's ethos.

In such a small school (22 on roll) there is frequent contact with children and staff in other classes. We sit together over lunch and discuss each other's activities, interests, successes and upsets. The promotion of self-esteem of the children, team members and myself is central to my practice and has been a theme throughout the discussion. It is my responsibility as a whole-school team member, as it is of all other members, to our caring ethos.

'Behaviour in school is known to be related to the general atmosphere, ethos or climate of the school.'[16] Rutter et al (1979)[17] found the ethos of successful schools to include teachers with the following qualities: acting as positive role models; having high expectations of their pupils; and providing effective feedback on appropriate behaviour.

In this paper I have explored the various ways and means by which I endeavour to exercise my contractual accountability to play my part in the 'education' of individuals, to facilitate their academic and social growth. The creation of an understanding, secure and esteem-promoting environment, however, is intrinsic to access to the curriculum and the cornerstone of its effectiveness. The conducive 'conditions of learning' (particularly relationships) mentioned previously, and effective feedback on what is appropriate behaviour, combine with the other areas of responsibility explored to affect and reflect the school's ethos. On such a solid foundation my curriculum and assessment accountability are an intellectual challenge.

My practice is within a child-centred partnership between home, school and those providing education. Such a goal demands belief that it is attainable, and requires all the partners to undertake their accountabilities with honesty and commitment in its pursuance. It can, and has to be, 'catalysed' by us teachers ourselves. Time is precious, resources may be low, but if we want to maximise the educational opportunity for the children we have to organise the challenge.

References

1   DES *Special Educational Needs* (The Warnock Report), London, HMSO, 1978.
2   SEAC *Records of Achievement in Primary Schools*, HMSO, 1990.
3   Hewett, F.M. and Taylor, F.D. *The Emotionally Disturbed Child in the Classroom*, Boston, Allyn & Bacon, 1980.
4   London Borough of Hillingdon Education Department *5-16 Curriculum Policy Statement*, 1990.
5   McManus, M. *Troublesome Behaviour in the Classroom — A Teacher's Survival Guide*, New York/London, Routledge, 1989.
6   DES, op. cit.
7   NCC Circular No. 5 *Implementing the National Curriculum — Participation by Pupils with Special Educational Needs*, NCC May 1989.
8   London Borough of Hillingdon Education Department, op. cit.
9   National Union of Teachers, *Special Educational Needs and the National Curriculum*, London, 1990.
10 London Borough of Hillingdon Education Department, op. cit.
11 Greenfield, J., in London Borough of Hillingdon Education Services *Records of Achievement 5-19*, Hillingdon Assessment Team, 1990.
12 London Borough of Hillingdon Education Services *Records of Achievement 5-19*, Hillingdon Assessment Team, 1990.
13 Ibid.
14 Ibid.
15 Moon, A. 'A Whole School Approach to Personal and Social Education with a Focus on Child Protection' in *Skills for the Primary School Child — The Manual*, Moon, A. (ed.), 1990.
16 McManus, M., op. cit.
17 Rutter, M., Maughan, B., Mortimore, P., and Ouston, J. *Fifteen Thousand Hours: Secondary Schools and Their Effects on Children*, London, Open Books, 1979.

4 Educational leadership

4.1 Embodying the school

Maggie Pringle

There was an American politician who, at moments of crisis, was heard to comfort himself by murmuring the words 'this, too, will pass'. A sense of proportion should not be undervalued. Schools seem to run on fairly high-octane fuel and a head who knows, for example, that this year's re-decoration programme is not likely to be more disruptive than the asbestos removal of three years ago — or, that an apparent rise in incidents of poor behaviour among pupils can be attributed at least in part to an over-ambitious programme of in-service training and therefore of cover of classes by supply teachers, rather than to a general, inexplicable decline in school discipline — a head who knows these, I suggest, plays a vital role in giving a context for those daily alarums and excursions of school life, which should be given due attention but no more. These, too, will pass. The skill lies in judging how much attention is due. The danger lies in elevating 'managing the turbulence' into an end in itself.

Schools, like classrooms, will always generate activity. Just as a class can be occupied with busy but ultimately unpurposeful work, so schools and heads can be kept virtuously busy in activity that lacks co-ordination and purpose. New activities keep us even more virtuously busy. A glance at my diary for next week indicated the extent to which my 'new' activities are occasioned by the imminent arrival of local management (LMS): it also shows that, however new the activity, the head still seems to be placed firmly in the middle of conflicting interests, a highly familiar place to most of us. One example is illustrative: we must, I am assured, 'sort out' the issue of shared use of the building. (The school is used extensively outside school hours by the adult education college on weekday evenings and by two community youth groups at the weekend.) The school's administrative officer and the deputy head (finance) have been toiling away at producing the cost per hour of leasing a room — a cost which strikes me as prohibitively expensive but which, they assure me, is nothing compared to a 'proper' commercial letting. Meanwhile, the organisations concerned seek to press their claims with me, reminding me of past commitments to their cause. Clearly, an individual school cannot be expected to bear the cost of the generous position that was once held by the largest education authority in the country. At the same time, one would hope to reach a position a little more complex than that of listening to the ring of the cash register. That sentence itself does an injustice to one side of the argument. 'To whom are we accountable?' urge the voices within the school. 'To the pupils. A proper lettings policy will generate income of direct benefit to the pupils.' The head who seeks the moral high ground — and which of us does not? — will do well to remember the words of John Donne:

> On a huge hill, rugged and steep,
> Truth stands and he that will
> Reach her, about must, and about must go. (Satire 3)

Our journey will be similarly fraught.

It may be argued that we have gone a considerable journey in my last paragraph, trying to see the apparently simple task of costing school lettings in the context of moral high grounds. I make no apology, for it is my belief that too many apparently every-day decisions in schools are made without reference to the school's principles and purposes.

My theoretical position about managing the constant flux of school life is to argue for shared purposes deriving from explicit principles. I was late in acknowledging how important it is that purposes and principles be made explicit. I should have known better, particularly after an illuminating incident at a former school. While we had all noticed a deterioration in behaviour amongst a group of boys in the third year (Year 9), it was the head of the year who pointed out that in three central subject areas the head of department had chosen to 'set' pupils in the face of increasing class size. The boys regularly found themselves in a bottom set and were possibly behaving accordingly. The school's unwritten commitment to a large element of departmental autonomy had come into (hitherto unnoticed) conflict with the school's written but unrevisited commitment to mixed-ability organisation in the lower school. When the conflict was finally made visible, the departments concerned agreed to return to mixed-ability grouping with some additional staffing to reduce class size. That decision itself had to be made explicit and in turn became part of the school's staffing policy. Since staffing resources are by no means infinitely flexible, it had to be stated that the principle of supporting the policy of mixed-ability grouping had been given a priority in resourcing terms over other claims on such resources. It will be even more important under LMS to make such decisions and the reasons for them explicit.

Another example illustrates the need to make underlying principles known and shared. In a major inspection, we were asked to explain the principles behind the school's curriculum offer, particularly in Years 10 and 11, in which a large option system operated. History and geography were strong in the school and many pupils, not surprisingly, opted for both. Other subjects 'fought for existence' alongside them in the option blocks. The inspector pointed out that the curricular principles actually operating were those of free choice by pupils and the wish to protect already successful areas of the curriculum, neither of them as strong as the principle of a broad and balanced curriculum and the need to raise achievement across the whole of it.

I was delighted therefore to find at my present school the principles underpinning the curriculum agreed and written down. They are referred to when curriculum change or development is discussed. They have not needed to be changed as a direct result of the arrival of the National Curriculum — a timely reminder that the National Curriculum is not a school's whole curriculum. I have found, however, that a set of principles rarely leads to only one solution: it does, though, constantly inform the debate and it rules out certain options. It serves to strengthen in a school those things that make a difference and that make one school distinct from its neighbours.

My initial reluctance to make principles explicit had stemmed from the belief that secondary schools have so much in common that differences would seem negligible. Which school, after all, would not plead its commitment to achievement, its desire to enable all pupils to reach their full potential, its belief in an 'entitlement' curriculum? Did individuality then lie in the more visible features of a school, the things most clearly evident to parents: for example, we do not have a uniform, we do have a lot of computers. Each of these could become a starting point from which to explore the complex network of values and principles that makes each school unique, but we should not short-circuit that exploration by arguing, for example, that we have computers or a uniform 'because it is what parents want'. Having or not having a uniform is very closely related to the values of a school. It is not a marketing device.

Speaking of marketing, I had a chastening reminder that schools often make fairly simplistic assumptions about what parents want of a school. At a recent seminar entitled 'How to market your company more effectively' I was arguing, somewhat irritatingly, I am sure, that as I was in education and not in marketing, I had clearly been invited in error. An articulate, immaculately dressed young businessman assured me that if I ever wrote or spoke about my school in an attempt to describe its virtues and thus to persuade parents to choose it, then I was in the business of marketing. 'Why do you think it is a good school?' he asked with interest. As reluctant as I suspect many heads are to embark on definitions of the good school, I turned the tables and suggested that, as a parent, he should have ideas about the good school. He did.

He replied immediately and carefully that he knew exactly the kind of school that he wanted for his child: a school that offered a much broader curriculum than he had received at his school, a school that encouraged a sense of responsibility for society, and a school in which his child was educated alongside the broadest possible range of pupils from all backgrounds. If a parent can be that clear in defining the school he wants, then a head can be equally clear and indeed courageous in defining the school's aim.

The head must be equally clear and courageous in pointing out the extent to which the articulated principles of the school's aim are not finding expression in its practice. I am interested in how the head does that and believe that the answer lies in the interlocking concepts of role and authority. My own school has the aim statement: 'We want a school with more powerful students and more powerful staff.' In an educational climate in which very different kinds of people use words like 'entitlement', 'relevant' and even 'citizenship' with quite different resonances, we can be forgiven, I think, for having spent rather a long time discussing what we did — and did not — mean by 'powerful'. Whatever our problems with the word, it has remained central to our aim statement and a useful tool in guiding and informing many recent discussions and decisions.

I think I have been the person at school who has lived most intensely with the aim statement. It is appropriate then that I have been the one to articulate the feeling that our curriculum offer — impressively broad and balanced as it is — reflects the aim much more in theory then in practice. In short, there is quite a gap between what I perceive as actually happening in the upper school curriculum and what the aim statement suggests is intended to happen. I have outlined the following perceived disadvantages of our curriculum, as it is received by pupils: it does not guarantee differentiation as all pupils follow largely the same route; it leaves the responsibility for the learning too much with the teacher and not sufficiently with the pupils; as a two-year 'journey' it lacks pace and is altogether too leisurely. None of these conclusions has been scientifically arrived at although I believe they can all be defended. They could be called almost entirely subjective although, as I shall suggest later, there is evidence available to support them.

When I reflect how defensive teachers have become about their own practice and how much they have come to expect criticism from outside rather than from within, I cannot but think that my comments have been well received. However, I began with certain advantages: after five years as head, I can hardly be criticised as an impetuous and insensitive new broom, crassly sweeping away that which it was not bothered to understand. However, with a sympathetic nod to those heads who do not feel that they can wait for five years, I wish to explore what has given me the authority to make my critique of our curriculum offer.

One factor sounds reassuringly scientific and objective, so I shall mention it first: schools are full of evidence about their performance which is known best to those working within them and which they have not been empowered to use. Attendance and punctuality figures, exam entries as well as exam results, staying-on rates, pupils' involvement in extra-curricular activities, the results of classroom observation, surveys of pupils' attitudes, work experience reports from employers: these are just a handful of the kinds of evidence schools could look at. They are the tools of that sensible process which the Inner London Education Authority, so many years ago, called 'keeping the school under review'. They should be the kinds of material that a school looks at, searchingly and openly, to assess its performance. It is a cause for considerable regret that 'performance indicators' have come to be seen by many teachers as the 'searchlight from outside', the tool of, not the critical friend, but the critical outside observer, who does not understand the rules of the game but freely condemns the players. The temptation is to find as quickly as possible an answer to a difficult question. An inspector looking at our exam entries statistics, asked why such a relatively high percentage of our pupils did not enter for examinations in the core subjects. After a good deal of research, the head of year with some relief came up with what she saw to be the answer: that a significant number of pupils joined the school well into the 10th and 11th year. I had to point out (tactfully, I hope) that this answer itself merely pointed to a new question: 'What does the school do to support those pupils who join the school in the 10th and 11th years in entering for examinations?'

The recognition that the search for improvement has been relocated rather than closed down comes, I think, from the central principle of accountability to pupils. You investigate the evidence about pupil achievement in order to identify the real questions, not to find easy answers.

It was the combination of re-focusing on the aim statement and looking at pieces of school-generated evidence that led us in determining the four priorities for our last school development plan. On a professional development day, all staff — teachers and support staff — did exercises designed to identify the strengths and weaknesses of the school in relation to the aim statement. Only after these were followed through did staff move on to articulate their priorities for the next two years. The senior team met in a high-pressured 45 minutes to identify four central themes from all the ideas submitted by all the groups. We did not really expect to be taken unawares by the groups' findings, nor did we approach the exercise cynically with the view that we would easily match the findings to our pre-conceived set of priorities. We have to be prepared to loosen the mechanisms of control in order to release the energy available in an institution. We also have to realise that, if the staff's priorities match hardly at all with those of the senior team, then the school is in real difficulties!

But of course the links are there between the perceptions of the school's priorities held by the head, the senior team and the staff. And those links are there because of what I can only call the art (or is it the act?) of embodiment, by which I mean a head's ability to draw upon the experience of the school, to feel the experience of a pupil joining mid-way through the 10th year, to understand the defensiveness of a teacher who always seems to oppose change, to embody in short the aspirations, values and experiences of those who have a stake in the school — governors, parents, pupils and staff — and also those who visit it, work with it or make judgements about it from outside.

Such a process does not lead, as might at first appear likely, to a dissipation of the head's own integrity. (To understand everyone's point of view could be seen as leading to a total paralysis of action.) It is almost the reverse; the process of embodiment, of managing a constant dialogue with different groups with a stake in the school, leaves the head more confident in making judgements, particularly those that relate to managing the middle ground between conflicting interests. For example, I am currently working on a set of guidelines relating to personnel procedures, including monitoring staff absence, applications for leave of absence, special leave and so on. I have made it clear that I am trying to give due consideration to three sometimes conflicting principles: considerate treatment of individual staff, equitable treatment of all staff and our accountability to our pupils. The very stating of the principles plus the shared recognition that they will at times conflict makes decisions easier, not more difficult.

It may be argued at this stage that I have said disappointingly little about the changes in the head's role brought about by the Education Reform Act, 1988. I have attended the LMS seminars given by the new breed of consultants. I have gone through the 33 (or was it 38?) new statutory responsibilities laid upon heads now without the comforting words, 'the head will endeavour within reason to . . .'. Apparently now we just will. I've made an impressive list of the policies I need to draft for the governors: staffing policy, salaries policy, disciplinary policy, grievance policy. I have drawn diagrams showing the respective roles of the head, governing body and the local education authority, all in boxes, with arrows flying back and forth in bewildering fashion. Just as the diagram of the carefully labelled cow that I drew as a pupil in home economics never quite resembled what I saw in the butcher's shop, so these diagrams never quite unpick the reality of working with governors or with the LEA. For entirely understandable reasons I think we have probably laid too much emphasis recently on our contractual and financial responsibilities, on the statutory powers of parents, governors, teachers, heads, officers, elected members and advisers and have rather neglected a worthwhile discussion about the qualities of headship that will enable a head to work with them.

The law must be worked with, not merely known and understood. I remember some while ago having a disagreement over the practical interpretation of a governor's duty to have oversight of the curriculum. I felt the governor's interpretation encroached upon the LEA's duty to inspect, she felt that what she was doing fell within the guidance for governors from the National Association of Governors and Managers. I hurried to a legal adviser for help and was assured cheerfully that this was a grey area that would one day need to be resolved by a court case. I felt decidedly less cheerful about the prospect than he did.

To return to the diagrams and the boxes: as I contemplate the box marked 'head', I find it much more helpful to think of myself not as taking over a list of powers and responsibilities, but as taking up a role, and in that role engaging with others also taking up a role. It is always helpful to be reminded that, as head, governor or LEA member or officer, one is taking up a role and has to know the scope of it. I constantly admire the skill with which parent governors fulfil their role, knowing that they represent a large and diverse constituency, a fraction of whom elected them and a fraction of whom they meet at the annual meeting to present the governors' report to parents. They too know about embodiment.

I was very impressed recently by an experienced head who urged his audience of headteachers never to support a decision or course of action by the weasel excuse of 'I'm doing it because I have to as part of my contract'. I have been guilty of it — just as I have also been guilty of using the excuse 'It will be the governors' decision, not mine'. It is not that the reason is not accepted: quite the reverse, teachers are often very sympathetic to it. It is rather that, in setting up the idea of a head whose role is constrained by the legal and contractual framework, it actually undercuts the whole process I have outlined above, in which the head seeks to embody the values and aspirations of all those with a stake in the school, seeks to work with them all in defining the aim statement, seeks to use it as a tool in informing decision-making and does it all with an openness that says 'I took this decision because I believed it to be right for these reasons'. Such a process has the great value of being a motivator for empowerment throughout the school. We all have to be empowered and enabled to make decisions.

We recently had to make a choice about a major investment in computer hardware. (I noted with interest, by the way, that, at a seminar in which heads were asked to analyse the stages and factors in a decision they had made recently, 90 per cent of them spoke with anxiety of choosing hardware.) Back at school, the management group of senior post-holders was augmented by the information technology advisory group of enthusiastic, knowledgeable and (generally) younger teachers. We had the advice of inspectors, advisory teachers and LEA officers. We made phone calls to any friend, relative or other contact who could possibly advise us. You could almost feel the anxiety and indeed reluctance with which the group approached its decision. We called for more reports, more information, more advice. We might still have been discussing (and indeed delaying) the decision even now, had one member of the group not given us the confidence to take the decision by pointing out that we, the group that took the decision, would also take ownership of it and work with it; that, having responsibility for it, we would recognise that no decision would be absolutely right, that no computer system is the entirely perfect answer and that the best hope of making our decision work lay in our own commitment to it. We were empowered.

I have described the process in some detail since it has seemed to me to be almost a change in direction from a phenomenon which I have noticed with sadness over the past years and which I will describe as the phenomenon of teachers as victims.

The word is melodramatic but it will serve. It is not merely that central government has made so many decisions closely affecting teachers' working lives. It is not merely that teachers have felt themselves to be undervalued and indeed criticised on all sides. It is also felt that they have lost some conviction of their power — or, to put it better, of the authority of their role as teachers. And the centrality of that role cannot be under-estimated. I was recently a member of a group that considered a number of crucial activities within school (such as monitoring pupils' progress) with the purpose of determining who was ultimately accountable for them. The vast majority of the answers identified either the head or the classroom teacher — a recognition of the centrality of the teacher managing the complex systems and interactions of the classroom.

Yet we all find it easy to lose touch with the authority of our role. We give more power than we need to gods, dragons and — dare I say — nanny figures outside. 'The Authority', I still hear teachers say — and note the use of the word authority — 'The Authority must . . .' or 'The Authority will . . .' and I still have to point out that, under LMS, not only will we have the authority to do the particular thing under discussion, but, because of the changing role of the LEA, if we don't do it, it will not be done.

That perception is liberating — it is also challenging. In my school, having worked for a large, powerful and intervening LEA, we now work for a very small one that seeks to delegate a wide range of decisions and responsibilities and that seeks to re-examine the relationship of the school and the LEA.

I do not seek to deny the constraints that operate upon individual schools: constraints that relate to resources, to geographical location, to pupil intake — to a whole range of factors. Nor do I minimise the very real fears about local management of schools. 'We shall soon know the price of everything and the value of nothing', lamented one teacher who felt that English was being given more curricular time in his school because, as subjects go, it is deemed 'cheap to run'.

The positive features of LMS are that schools will need to look firstly within themselves for strength and expertise. They will need genuinely participative decision-making processes in which the responsibility for implementing decisions is just as important as the right to be involved in making them. They will find, I hope, that while the LEA's role will change, it will still be a source of support, in the form of information, advice and resources when needs and opportunities can be demonstrated. Most important of all, my hope is that if teachers can be empowered to take up their role with a greater conviction of its authority, then they will be successful in empowering pupils to take up their role more effectively too.

5 Quality in education

5.1 Evaluation for improvement
Del Goddard

Teachers have power over the pupils they teach. For this reason it is both right and necessary that teachers and the education service are accountable to the community for the quality of provision. In return, society has the responsibility to know what it wants the education service to be accountable for and to know how to hold it accountable.

Quality is difficult to pin down. But however it is defined it can be achieved only by the improvement of learning and teaching in schools and classrooms. How to do this remains contentious: the direction of education (the curriculum) is the subject of a continuing debate. Regrettably there is little discussion or research about the way children learn and thus how they might be taught.

There is an alliance between teachers and society that inhibits professional debate and development on improving education. Engineers, doctors, scientists all seek to improve the stock of knowledge and skill that underpins their work. In education the absence of a strong professional base of understanding about learning and teaching means that teachers are left relatively unskilled: politicians and the public, from whatever base of experience, feel free to enter into the debate on teaching. Assertion and counter-assertion have little rational or empirical base. Of late the education debate has almost deliberately been taken out of the professional and empirical parameters. (Consider for a moment the reaction from the public and the doctors if the Secretary of State for Health was to pronounce on the best way for a doctor to treat cancer.) The consequence is that the confidence of teachers has been eroded, as has the confidence of the community, the parents, business and the politicians in the system.

In this chapter I examine what is meant by quality, discuss its improvement through effective development and finally relate it to evaluation and accountability.

Quality in education
What is quality? Behind the question lies the debate about the purpose of education. Three extracts, many years apart, serve to illustrate the continuing debate within society. The first is from Herbert Read:

But it is not likely that I shall carry general agreement on the purpose I ascribe to education, for here there are at least two irreconcilable possibilities: one, that man should be educated to become what he is not. The first view assumes that each individual is born with certain potentialities which have a positive value for that individual and that it is his proper destiny to develop these potentialities within the framework of a society liberal enough to allow for an infinite variation of types. The second view assumes that whatever idiosyncrasies the individual may possess at birth, it is the duty of the teacher to eradicate them unless they conform to a certain ideal of character determined by the traditions of the society of which the individual has involuntarily become a member.[1]

A stark contrast. Yet every teacher seeks daily to reconcile the two positions.

The second extract is from the British Standards Institute:

Quality has a number of different meanings but B.S.5750 looks at it through the fitness for purpose . . . is the service provided designed and constructed to satisfy the customer's needs?[2]

There is no absolute in this definition. There is no immediate help for the education service as it does not help us to define standards nor, for that matter, does it clarify the educational customer. Is it society, the employer, the parent or the pupil? How do you reconcile the National Curriculum with the needs of the individual?

The third extract is from *Total Quality Management*:

. . . Quality then is simply meeting the customer requirements, tempered by the concept of reliability — to function satisfactorily over a period of time.[3]

There is difficulty in the application of industrial models where physical specification is feasible and desirable, or from a true service industry where the needs of the customer can be defined one-dimensionally.

Quality is the product of two processes. One is the debate about what has to be taught. The second is the establishment of a learning environment for the student, the staff and the service. Student achievement is the product of both. These two processes will be examined in greater detail later. In education, a statement of quality in terms of the achievement of the ability to learn and the need to reach agreement may be too bald for many to accept. In many walks of life it is the product that matters, but product outcome cannot be guaranteed in education. Every child has the right to education, and it is impossible to determine the quality of intake to ensure quality of outcome.

Listening to debates on education one is struck by the demand for agreement about quality as defined by the skills that young people need. The list is fairly obvious: those skills that can be defined as 'basic' (numeracy and language), personal skills and a number of others like problem-solving. Even so, there is still a lack of agreement as to the full range required. There is even more disagreement about content, which is why the process of agreeing what is to be taught is so fundamental. Even with a national curriculum, society has not found a satisfactory way to do this. There is little wrong with the concept of a broad national framework that has been fully and properly discussed between all the partners. National Curriculum developments in many countries point to the setting of the main framework nationally and decentralisation of the substance of the curriculum. The absence of a truly national and local arrangement leaves the education service without meaningful goals. The complexity of society, and thus of the goals of education, has to be addressed in the debate on direction and content. Sufficient agreement to achieve effective action is central to the determination and achievement of quality. Imposed curricula are unlikely to be effective.

Quality in education comes from partnership. It rests on collaboration and the creation of confidence, so that each partner can learn how to improve. It is progressively built up from broad national, even international (EEC) statements of aims by LEAs, schools, colleges and individual teachers.

Quality and accountability

Accountability appears precise. As a principle it commands assent. In its managerial form, everyone assumes that it delivers quality. But does it? How does it contribute to the motivation of the profession? In education means and ends are very closely associated. Appropriate accountability methods (means) are therefore critical to achieving quality (ends). At present, society, through its politicians, is pursuing a crude and coercive form of accountability that will demotivate and deskill teachers and thus fail to achieve improved quality. Working collaboratively to solve a problem is not characteristic of the current political approach.

I wish now to consider a number of ideas about accountability, to examine the relationship between various forms and discuss the ways in which different mixes do or do not produce improvement.

'Accountability must be associated with feelings of responsibility. When people feel accountable they attempt unconsciously to improve their performance. When people feel unfairly called to account they devise ways of beating the accountancy without actually improving the balance sheet.'[4]

This raises questions about the value of the traditional inspection report. Such a report has to be both professionally respected and accepted. It is not an agent of accountability or an aid to improvement if its recommendations are rejected by head, staff and governors. Improvement comes from actions that are based on feelings of responsibility.

'Schools' accountability rests on understandings, not decisions.'[5]

Effective action by teachers, schools, the governors or LEAs stems from committed understanding. Understanding that is superficial or insufficient fails to guide real change and improvement. The process of evaluation (including inspection or appraisal) has to be integrated with the processes of improvement and learning at both the individual and institutional level. Evaluation that does not increase insight and understanding is unable to inform either.

Three forms of accountability can be distinguished:

'moral accountability — being answerable to clients and customers (students and parents);
professional accountability — being responsible to oneself and colleagues; and
contractual accountability — being accountable to one's employers.'[6]

In education there is a constant tension between these accountabilities which the Education Reform Act 1988 has both sharpened through its legislative approach and extended by formulating national requirements and increasing the powers of governing bodies.

A simple map of accountability cannot be drawn. It is not secured through successive grades from pupil to government even though the legislation would seem to imply that.

The concept of downwards (moral) accountability to the student flows from the relationship of the teacher to the child. Many teachers are motivated directly by this responsibility to children, especially those in primary schools, even when this is counterbalanced by dominant pressures for upwards (contractual) accountability to meet curriculum and managerial goals.

Professional accountability remains the weakest of the three forms of accountability, yet it probably has more to contribute to quality than the others. High quality teaching demands increasing professional examination. For too long that has been denied to the profession along with the means to research its understanding of the learning process. The increasing prescription of the National Curriculum and the coercive characteristics of schemes of evaluation, inspection, teacher appraisal, pupil assessment and exam tables create pressure without providing real information either to the profession or the public about the state of education and the means of its improvement. The consequent loss of confidence within the profession may explain the shift from society's trust of moral and professional accountability to a more contractual arrangement. Whether or not this confidence was well placed in the past, the danger is that contractual accountability becomes a self-fuelling process that destroys other more effective forms. The resulting unbalanced mix fails to improve or even maintain quality. Public or political security may stem temporarily from contractual accountability, but when this is at odds with the teachers' feelings of responsibility to students and colleagues the tension is destructive.

Confidence and quality are more likely when contractual accountability is the safety net, professional accountability the support and moral accountability the driving force. Together they make the structure. Together they provide the means for dealing with the unacceptable, for solving problems, for developing teachers and schools and restoring the confidence and morale of the service and the public. Each accountability on its own is inadequate. Lay persons may not know whether something has been properly done until it goes wrong. In education this is even more crucial as outcomes take several years to emerge. Education is continuous and its outcomes long-term. It is unwise to wait for years to find that a pupil's or school's standards are low. Contractual accountability is too crude and too late. Continuous accountability is essential if quality is to be maintained and improved.

A further consideration in the balance of accountabilities is to recognise which elements have to remain confidential and those that have to be made public. This is not to hide problems, but to achieve effectiveness. Make everything public and the service will opt for safety and standards will fall. Reduce the information and society will lose trust, confidence and the means to share in agreeing what needs to be done. The profession needs confidential circumstances where ideas can be tried, doubts and differences discussed. Without that, educational advancement will cease.

The current danger is that the balance and methods of accountability are too crude and are likely to produce a system of evaluation that will fail. A thorough re-examination of the roles of teachers, governors, parents, communities, LEAs and government, in evaluation, appraisal, inspection, professional development and the means of agreeing curriculum and assessment is needed to arrive at a working partnership that restores confidence and enhances quality. We need to strengthen all three forms of accountability and to create an effective balance between them.

Quality and learning

An effective balance of accountabilities does not of itself assure quality. The process of achieving and improving quality is a learning process for every member of the service, not just the student. The continuous professional development of teachers drives the process, yet its contribution to quality is barely recognised. This singularly English failure can be seen throughout society in the way it resources and values all forms of education and training. The significance of the demand that all teachers should remain learners lies in the relationship of teacher and student. For young people to be effective learners, their teachers have to be learners as well. The creative construction of the learning experience requires teachers continuously to reflect both on the pupils' progress and on their own teaching. Quality teaching is continuously creative.

Effective pupil learning depends not just on classroom practice, but on the way in which the teacher is supported as a learner by the service as a whole. The school is a learning organisation that provides students, teachers and parents with an environment created and maintained by the public authorities.

Not only is teacher learning central to effective teaching but it is vital in the development and delivery of a quality curriculum. Such a curriculum can never be totally prescribed. A national framework always needs substance and modification. With the curriculum, as with other things, to adopt one must adapt.

Curriculum is not static: it changes and needs to match the needs of individuals and society.

To be translated into student achievement, the curriculum has to be organised and designed into student experiences. This is a creative process where quality depends on the full commitment of the teacher and the school. There are few parallels in other areas of work. The curriculum is not like a ready-made meal that can be packaged at some distant factory and remain untouched until cooked and consumed, though this is a model that many still claim to have in mind: the teacher-proof curriculum, designed by a grand architect and technically delivered in the classroom. The teacher is both the architect and the builder. Curriculum design, teaching and learning are one complex and dynamic process, which requires the active mental, physical and emotional involvement of the teacher.

A further feature of effective teaching is the teachers' understanding and practice of their pedagogical skills, management capabilities and knowledge of the educational context.

The professional development of teachers (learning for teachers) is an essential component in quality. It interrelates the needs of the individual teacher with the challenges of the job. The motivation of teachers to remain learners and to engage in professional, staff, institutional and curriculum development throughout their careers underpins professional accountability and ensures responsibility.

Evaluation and improvement

> Evaluation is a general term used to describe any activity where the quality of the provision is subject to systematic study.

> It involves the collection, analysis, interpretation and reporting of evidence about the nature, impact and value of the entity.

> Thus monitoring, review and assessment are aspects of evaluation if systematic analysis of data is used to provide information for decisions.[7]

There are various terms used in the debate on evaluation, especially on the inspection of schools: *quality control,* which is simply a policing function; *quality assurance,* which is concerned with the achievement of quality; and *quality development,* which I take to mean the improvement of the standard.

Educational evaluation should be about quality assurance and quality development, quality control operating at agreed levels. As with the appraisal of teachers, it is undesirable to construct a system that makes more of identifying the one per cent failures than improving the 99 per cent.

The current proposals for the inspection of schools lack clarity about purposes and the balance between quality control, assurance and development. If the balance swings too far towards control, assurance and development will be starved out. The consequence will be a decline in quality, as has happened in the USA.

The first purpose of evaluation is to inform the subject: evaluation for improvement. The second is to inform others.

The balance between these two purposes has been moved, as a result of the political and individual desire for choice, towards the provision of information for others to make decisions. The assumption is that it is desirable and feasible to specify the curriculum nationally in considerable detail and then to assess attainment against it. The quality of schools is defined by their ability to deliver the national specification. The strategy depends on the influence on a poor school either of falling numbers or of adverse inspection reports. It is a market model, but it is not the only one.

The question is whether the education service's understanding of learning, improvement and accountability demands another approach. The second purpose of evaluation — for improvement — is to generate the motivation of teachers and schools to develop their practice. Evaluation is part of learning and can only be defined and judged in these terms.

My confidence in the model that I propose below stems from a wide examination of evaluation and an understanding of the application of learning to improvement. There are principles which should inform the various processes of inspection, appraisal and assessment and practices which encourage learning and achievement.

A Norwegian once told to me that he found the differences in our two countries' health and safety arrangements very illuminating. He characterised the UK approach as the inspectorate visit to check on a particular date if everthing was satisfactory. It either was or was not. The Norwegian approach was to check whether the organisation took its responsibilities seriously and had evaluation in place. The role of the outsider was to work with the organisation to provide an external validation and to enhance and examine the ways in which it maintained its safety procedures.

The second approach secures responsibility for quality and improvement within a collaborative arrangement that is managed and operated by all the parties. In education these would be teachers in schools and colleges, governors (including parents and lay people) and the LEA on behalf of the community. The balance of accountabilities would be distributed, understood and agreed by all, so that quality may be sought and maintained. If partnership provides the basis for quality and improvement, partnership has to be at the heart of evaluation.

Evaluation for improvement is a continuous process, coupling pressure and support, to create motivation and learning — prerequisites for effective improvement.

If standards are to rise, the emphasis must be on quality assurance and development. Quality control and information to parents have a subordinate place. A different balance will lead at best to a standstill and at worst to deterioration.

Evaluation in the 1990s

Real improvement of quality requires the agreement and achievement of curriculum goals, development procedures and sound evaluation.

Effective learning underpins all aspects of the education service, especially the work of schools, teachers, governors and the LEA, perhaps in time of government itself. The touchstone of any arrangement for achieving quality is whether it enables all the parties to learn and to develop their understanding of education. Achieving quality and raising standards demands change, and change is a process of learning.

The current debate dusts off traditional models of inspection and places them within a model of market forces. It locates inspectors,

LEAs and governors within a framework of contractual account-ability and uses testing and inspection to reinforce this: set the target, appropriate or not, and see if it has been achieved. Education deserves something better, if the main promise of the Education Reform Act 1988 is to be realised. This is to ensure that all pupils are being educated satisfactorily, not just monitored or inspected.

The question is whether a system designed and predominantly resourced for quality control is capable of offering quality assurance and development, whether the procedures for quality control motivate the service to improve. Experience causes me to doubt this.

The private conviction of those directly involved, especially head-teachers, teachers and inspectors is that inspection reports rarely lead to desired improvement of the subject concerned. Contractual co-ercion is not effective with most teachers since they are driven by their concern for pupils. This moral accountability needs reinforcing through evaluation that the teachers build into their work: watching children, looking at how they learn and changing practice according-ly. Quality of attainment remains the product of the teaching-learn-ing relationship. Evaluation has to focus upon it, in a way that makes the teacher learn from the information that it produces.

The failure to locate inspection within sound evaluation and a framework for improvement weakens inspection and assessment. Inspection should lie within an evaluation procedure which itself should be a continuous, integral, conscious and systematic engine of improvement. It should reinforce both moral and professional responsibility.

An interlinked education service provides the student with teach-ing and support from the teacher and the school, with the LEA supporting both. The object is to emphasise moral accountability to pupils, parents and the community within a professional framework. Contractual accountability is held both by the profession and the employer as necessary.

Four evaluative elements are required. First is a sound institutional evaluation, located within a professional framework of integral sup-port and external moderation. It links with professional account-ability and enhances responsibility and understanding.

Second is openness to parents, governors and the public which brings together professional and contractual accountability. Again this should lead to understanding and responsibility for all those involved.

The third element is the means to deal satisfactorily with the unacceptable, either within a confidential or public arena.

The fourth element is information about the quality of the school. There is a difficulty here; raw data rarely constitute information. A car may be going at 50 mph. This fact is useless out of context: it becomes information when one also knows that the car is on a motorway or in a built-up area. In other words, information has to be presented for a purpose and with an audience in mind. Information for parents is one purpose. Information for professionals for the purposes of improvement is another. What is required is for the data collected for evaluation procedure to be re-presented to inform parents. It does not work the other way round. Raw figures for comparative purposes are unsatisfactory in themselves and useless for any substantial evaluation for improvement.

The argument can be tested against the assumption by Stenhouse[8] that accountability is concerned with the generation of the feeling and operation of responsibility. Evaluation that is primarily concerned with information to parents and the system is likely to be cautious and incomplete.

Confidence in evaluation stems from a mix of skill, knowledge and understanding, coupled with a genuine belief that the processes will not be damaging. Accountability, including evaluation, inspection and improvement, must be sound learning experiences. Learning is sometimes painful, but the balance must not be destructive.

Four types of review together meet the various purposes for evaluation: school self-evaluation; specific review; whole-school inspection; and LEA survey.

School evaluation

The purpose of self-evaluation is to build the school's capacity for improvement through its own rigorous internal scrutiny. The procedures should be integral to the school's development and planning. Self-evaluation should complement the work on teacher appraisal for professional development and foster collaborative projects amongst staff that focus on practice. The Open University's 'Classroom in Action' pack and other similar materials provide sound starting points for schools and staff. Most, if not all, schools require help with self-evaluation, which in turn provides the framework for specific reviews and whole-school inspections.

Specific review

The purpose of this review is to provide the school and LEA with judgement on specific areas of work, for example, mathematics teaching or the administration of the budget. Specific review should be linked to self-evaluation and arise out of a school's development programme.

The significant features of specific review are that it takes place at a time that the school determines; is part of a development programme; contains an external professional report; and includes such items as internal self-evaluation documents and reports of moderators, advisers and inspectors, including HMI.

Whole-school inspection

This would be a periodic, preferably three-year, inspection of the school as a whole. It would draw on the other forms of review and be concerned with both the achievements of the school and practice of management and evaluation. The agenda for the inspection would be drawn up following discussion with all the parties concerned. The final report would be presented to the governors and the LEA and would be published.

LEA survey

The purpose of this survey is to inform the LEA on the state of the service so that it can undertake its statutory functions for resource management, policy and teacher development. Survey information may well be drawn from the other forms of review, but specific visits by the local inspectorate are likely to be needed to inform judgement. The information gathered would be available to the school.

This pattern of review meets all the purposes of evaluation listed above. Grounded in an improvement process, undertaken according to sound evaluation procedures, it provides for both improvement and information for others. Such an integrated approach to evaluation and improvement is the mark of an effective school, LEA and governing body. It assumes that each contributor to the process is both a teacher and a learner. For it to function effectively the LEA has to establish a positive local environment. Neither the governing body nor market forces can hold staff to professional account. The student is powerless and contractual accountability is inadequate.

Quality depends on a learning environment that locates evaluation and inspection within a model of improvement, where all the contributory processes become complementary, where energy in people and the system can be released and where efficiency and effectiveness manifest themselves in a system in harmony.

References

1   Read, H., *Education through Art* 3rd Edn, Faber and Faber, London, 1950.
2   BS 5750/ISO 9000: 1987, *A Positive Contribution to Better Business*, BSI Quality Assurance on behalf of DTI.
3   Department of Trade and Industry, *Total Quality Management: A Practical Approach*.

4   Stenhouse, L., 'Educational Accountability and Support for
    Teachers', *Times Educational Supplement*, 13th May 1977.
5   Nias, J., 'The Nature of Trust', Elliot J. *School Accountability*
    Blackwell, Oxford, 1981.
6   Bush, T. (Ed.), *Approaches to School Management*, Harper and Row,
    London, 1980.
7   Eraut, M., 'Institution-based Curriculum Evaluation' in Skilbeck, M.,
    Evaluating the Curriculum in the Eighties, Hodder and Stoughton,
    1984.
8   Stenhouse, L., op. cit.

6 School management

6.1 Theory and practice
Pat Petch

There are two ways of treating the management of schools. The first is to set out the theoretical roles, responsibilities and accountabilities of those involved in managing: the second is to deal with the reality of the situation. In many schools there is both confusion and concern about how these theoretical roles and responsibilities could and should operate in practice. It is one thing to talk in theory about the responsibility and accountability of governors since the Education Reform Act 1988, but it is another to do the job in a way which meets those obligations without coming into conflict with the head's perception of his or her role as a manager. The issue is who does what. Both heads and governors may feel that some matters fall within their territory, and encroachment is not welcome. There is the difficulty of agreeing how the traditional role of the head as decision maker fits in with the responsibility of governors for policy. There is the thorny issue of the role of 'amateurs' in a world of 'professionals'. We all know these problems exist and that they create tensions, but we find it hard to talk about them.

Increasingly, heads and governors are being required to give information about what they do and how well they do it. Parents and the wider community now have the right to detailed information. Those with information tend to ask questions. I believe that governors and heads will not have confidence when thus called to account, unless they have resolved the tensions which exist between them. We happily discuss the many beliefs we share as governors and heads — belief in the value of education, in the entitlement of children to quality and much more. We now need to acknowledge the relatively minor problems which cause working tensions and negotiate solutions acceptable to all. It may not be a comfortable debate, partly because we have avoided it for so long. It is essential if we aim to establish a relationship based on mutual trust within which we account confidently to one another and to the wider community.

What is school management?

We need to agree a definition of school management in order to agree our roles. For some, school management is defined in narrow terms: it covers the internal day-to-day running of the school, and is the concern of the head and staff alone. There is now another, wider, definition. As schools become genuinely self-managing, a wide range of decisions will rest within the school. Schools will have to establish and take responsibility for policies, when previously they simply received policies decided elsewhere and implemented them. A network of people — head, staff, governors, parents, the LEA and others both can and should be involved in the formulation of policy. I define school management as the network of people involved in decisions which ensure that policies have the consent of all affected by and contributing to them. Accountability arises through participation in the process of policy making, and participants are mutually accountable. It may be thought that this could never work in practice: it would take so long that policy would never emerge. But before dismissing this approach, let us consider the alternatives on offer.

Accountability and the market place

Much of the recent discussion about accountability has been in 'market' terms. In their report on local management of schools, Coopers and Lybrand[1] referred to the provisions of the Education Reform Bill as being designed to 'promote accountability and responsiveness of schools and their Local Education Authorities to their consumers'. Ever since, politicians and the media have continued to discuss education in terms of the need to ensure that 'schools' become effectively accountable to their 'consumers'. In translation 'consumer' usually means parent. It is interesting that children are hardly ever regarded as consumers of education. I have met many children, however, with clear views about education — what they expect, what they value, what they respect. They have many stimulating and challenging ideas about discipline, homework, the school environment, teaching and learning and much else. Children are rarely given a means through which they can articulate their views. Often, if some means exists such as a school council, children may describe it in private as a token gesture. They are aware that decisions have been made prior to consultation or that the agenda has effectively been set by others. We may say to one another that we are accountable to the child, but we make little effort to hear what children have to say. We should discuss the role of children in the processes and structures we will need if accountability is to become a reality.

Translation of the term 'school' is rather more difficult. We all tend to use the word 'school' quite a lot — but we use it in different ways at different times. Sometimes we mean the staff, sometimes the PTA and occasionally the site. In the accountability debate, teachers tend to think that 'the school' means them. Many teachers feel uneasy at an underlying tone of hostility in most of the political pronouncements on accountability. The suggestion is that all is not well in our schools and that the only way to put it right is to make 'the school' — in other words the teachers — answerable to parents.

The personal and professional accountability of teachers for their relationships and classroom practice is but one of many threads of accountability within a school. A teacher is accountable to the children, to parents, to colleagues, to the head, to governors and to the LEA. However, the market approach to accountability seems to centre on the teacher's relationship with the 'consumer' and to overlook the rest. My difficulty with this approach to accountability in education is that I find no evidence that it improves the quality of relationships, or even the quality of the product. Market accountability tends to be marked by confrontation rather than co-operation. Suppliers and consumers see themselves as separate groups and seldom co-operate to achieve a common end. There tends to be an emphasis on consumer rights, rather than consumer obligations. Dissatisfied buyers may put a supplier out of business, but they do not necessarily improve the quality of the product. An individual consumer may seek to call a supplier or manufacturer to account by making a complaint. If lucky, one gets a replacement or refund. If not, one is faced with the need to express increasing dissatisfaction and to threaten further action. A consumer is probably not concerned about the long-term relationship with the supplier. A consumer of education (sometimes known as a parent) will be concerned about the quality of the relationship with those providing education. Parents who are hostile, who demand accountability in market terms rarely feel satisfied in the end.

It is very easy to demand accountability, to write documents promising accountability, even to draft legislation requiring accountability. It is not so easy to achieve effective accountability in practice. Success or failure depends on attitudes. If people feel that what is required is fair, that it is part of a two-way process which recognises their views and values, that it is worthwhile, that the aim is to improve the service rather than threaten the individual, then they will be prepared to answer questions, share information and discuss what they are doing and why and how they are doing it. They will be prepared to help establish processes which lead to accountability and then participate in ways which ensure it is genuine. If people feel threatened, if they feel that their views do not matter or that it is not worthwhile, any process to make them accountable will be a token. Successful accountability can enhance the quality of relationships: token accountability may damage them, as people become resigned, disappointed or hostile. The consumer route to accountability in education is dangerous. Fortunately we can reject confrontation and develop through co-operation. A more constructive route lies through partnership and mutual accountability.

Partnership, mutual accountability and the no-change pessimist

Many schools describe the relationship between those involved in the life of a school as a 'partnership', but who are the partners, and what are their roles, rights and obligations? It is quite usual to refer to both parents and governors as working in partnership with the head and staff. I suspect that a traditional partnership model operates in many schools: everyone except the head and staff are sleeping partners who are required to nod in agreement after decisions have been made. Sometimes only the head and senior staff are active in deciding. As many have found, a sleeping partner remains responsible and accountable, even without participating in the activities of the enterprise. Suddenly, if things go wrong, all partners are called to account.

Governors have always had serious responsibilities. In most LEAs they have been legally responsible for 'the general direction and conduct of the school' for many years. The obligations placed on governors could be found in articles of government, and many articles set out extensive duties. In practice, however, governors were less than effective, partly because of the practice of 'grouping' many schools with a single governing body, partly because of the practice of political appointment and partly through want of use. There were few effective processes through which governors could be held accountable. The Education (No.2) Act 1986 provided a framework for both partnership and accountability, by controlling the use of grouping, establishing governing bodies with varied representation, including parents and staff, and establishing the annual report to parents and the annual meeting through which the governing body could be called to account.

At present the governors' annual meeting with parents is dismissed by many as a waste of time. In many schools turnout is low and parent interest lower. In many cases the invitation to the meeting is attached to a report which is either dense and turgid or so skimpy that it is hard to see why a meeting is required at all. Before issuing their first report, many governing bodies received guidance about the required content. In order to play safe and meet the requirements, governing bodies worked their way through the list and the end result was unlikely to generate much interest or understanding. Some still work in this way, others now produce lively and accessible reports.

There is also the issue of what actually happens at the meeting. In some cases the chair dutifully plods through the report in an expectation that no-one will really want to discuss things that happened some time ago and now cannot be altered. Parents are more likely to attend if they can raise issues of current concern, and even more likely to do so if they can discuss future proposals. In many early meetings parents discovered that on many issues that concerned them most — class size, the ways in which children were grouped, and the size and quality of classrooms and other teaching spaces — the governors did not decide. Governors might assure parents that they would cajole and harass the LEA into providing, but parents quickly realised that there was not much point in attempting to call governors to account for decisions they did not make. Now things are different.

The Education Reform Act 1988 provides that 'it shall be the duty of the authority to put at the disposal of the governing body of the school a sum equal to the school's budget share for that year to be spent for the purpose of the school'. The governors are responsible for the budget: as it is public money, they must be accountable. They are accountable to the LEA through monitoring, audit and the application of financial regulations. They are also accountable to parents for decisions made about the use of resources through the annual report and meeting. Decisions about staffing levels, redecoration and much more are now the responsibility of governors. Parents may feel that it is now worthwhile to attend the annual meeting, because the governors will have made the decisions about the things that matter most to parents. Next year, if we have to increase class sizes, reduce the number of teachers or implement any other unpopular decision we shall not be able to blame the LEA: our fall-guy has disappeared. It is true that the Act also says that governors may delegate their budget powers to the head. But they may only delegate it: they remain responsible and answerable for it.

Under the 1988 Act governors have responsibilities for appointing, suspending and dismissing staff, for ensuring that the National Curriculum is implemented, for daily collective worship and religious education, for reporting to parents, for the charging policy — in fact for a whole range of policy issues. Some governors may decide to delegate responsibility for all policy-making to the school. Some governors have too many competing interests to get involved, and others resent the time required and complain if they have to go to more than one meeting a term. In some schools the clear expectation from the head is that policy-making will be the responsibility of 'the school', but it is unwise to assume now that governors will always support policy made in their name but without their participation and genuine consent. When policy concerns difficult issues and there may be conflicting views amongst parents, staff and governors, few governors will willingly be called to account for decisions they did not make and may not support. Some governors are elected by interest groups. Any governor is a governor first and a representative of an interest group second. Governors are not mandated delegates. But if the views of the parent or staff governors are not expressed and considered while policy is being made, those governors may find themselves unable to support policy either privately or publicly.

Despite the recent changes, then, processes and attitudes have remained the same. In the main, governors and parents are still passive recipients of 'school' decisions rather than active participants in decision-making. This form of partnership operates on the basis of market accountability, with separate groups making demands of one another, so I feel rather pessimistic about it. A different definition of partnership may lead to mutual accountability and increase the confidence of all partners in working together.

Partnership, mutual accountability and the eternal optimist

The Oxford dictionary defines a partner as a sharer or partaker. There are many parents and governors who would just love to be sharers and partakers. Contrary to what is feared by some in education, parents and governors do not want to take over the running of schools. Most have quite enough to do running their own lives, and they genuinely respect the professional expertise of the head and staff. But if the partners in a school — the staff, head, governors, parents, professional colleagues and friends — are to become sharers and partakers, there will need to be give and take, open attitudes, shared ideas and information, and a constructive approach.

Machiavelli wrote:

> There is nothing more difficult to carry out, nor more doubtful of success, nor more dangerous to handle, than to initiate a new order of things. For the reformer has enemies in all who profit by the old order, and only lukewarm defenders in all those who would profit by the new order. This lukewarmness arises partly from fear of their adversaries, who have law in their favour, and partly from the incredulity of mankind who do not truly believe in anything new until they have had actual experience of it.[2]

People always feel threatened by an attempt to initiate a new order of things. In a sharing partnership partners will have to concede territory. Schools can be very territorial about some matters, for example, the curriculum. Some may find it threatening to concede that curriculum policy could be debated in its formative stage by those outside the staffroom.

In debate partners may reveal their values, uncertainties and prejudices. Such a possibility would make anyone feel hesitant. In debate it may emerge that in some policy areas there are many more questions than answers, and that no answer may be entirely satisfactory. I wonder if some heads think it a sign of weakness to ask those around them for help. Traditionally teachers have been projected as people who know. Many heads feel their role is to tell governors about the problem and immediately present the solution or a limited range of acceptable alternatives. Problems do require professional expertise, but in our newly self-managing schools, many problems could usefully be addressed by a wide range of people, and the wider perspectives they bring could lead to a better solution. Such a solution would withstand objection better because it would arise out of debate and have built in support and consent.

Who is to initiate such a new order? Governors can try if they themselves believe in the strength and value of a shared partnership and if there is a willingness within the school to think anew and start afresh. The burden of initiation cannot rest on heads alone.

Four things are necessary for success: agreement arising out of open discussion about the role of each partner; general willingness to be open to new ideas and approaches, no matter who initiates them; sharing of information with clear and open lines of communication; and processes which enable each partner to fill statutory or agreed roles in decision-making.

It will take time to establish a new order which satisfies the expectations and lays to rest the fears of all the partners. The surest way to succeed is to start. The occasion to look afresh at roles is the next major decision in the school.

Mutual accountability through partnership and participation with confidence are possible in our school because of the way we work. This is not perfect: we are still working at it. Our partnership tends to develop and change in interesting ways as we respond to new ideas and changed circumstances. But the thing that never changes is that it is an open and shared decision-making process. Let me conclude with an example.

In our school we are currently reviewing our aims. As we moved into self-management, as we adapted to the National Curriculum and tried to preserve the wider curriculum, we felt it right to think again about our shared values and to state them clearly. We started at the annual meeting of governors with parents in 1991. The governors discussed a whole range of issues with parents. All staff attended and took part in the debate. We spent some time considering the obligations of the school to parents — what they were, how we could agree them, how they could best be expressed. We also talked about the obligations of parents to the school. Out of this meeting we set up two working parties, each made up of parents, governors and staff who volunteered to meet, discuss and record their suggestions for school and parent obligations. Each group agreed how, when and where to meet, and worked to an agreed realistic timescale. The draft 'obligations' documents were discussed at a special staff meeting and by parents at a meeting with staff and governors. They were sent to every parent for comment. The head also discussed the document fully with all the children. Many parents have taken the opportunity to talk it through with their children. The amended agreed statement came back to the annual meeting this year for discussion. It will be adopted as policy by governors at their next meeting. This document is now known as our Home-School Partnership. It sets out the school's aims along with the detailed working obligations staff, parents, children and governors all have to one another.

We have developed policy through joint staff, governor and parent working parties for a number of years. We have no committees of either the governing body or the staff. Working parties are set up either to consider the next priority in our development plan, or to respond to some new issue. We operate one strict rule. All draft documents must be available to all participants well in advance of any meeting. If documents and information are not available, we re-arrange the meeting. Debate is impossible and accountability negligible in the absence of information. As a governor working in this way I am accountable to parents, staff, the head, fellow governors and children — and they are accountable to me. We aim to develop ways of working which will make accountability both mutual and continuous, not simply to fulfil our statutory obligations but because we believe it enables us to provide the most effective environment in which teachers can teach and children can learn.

My support for partnership arises out of participation and consent. Policy may not always be an exact statement of what I would have drafted left to myself, but I have always had an opportunity to put my point of view at the stage of policy formation, to influence policy, to adapt policy where others agree it is right and to concede where others are right. The staff and head are strengthened by knowing that their work is supported through the understanding and consent of the parents and governors. And as a governor I am both confident and optimistic.

References

[1] Coopers and Lybrand, *Local Management of Schools — A Report to the Department of Education and Science*, HMSO, London 1988
[2] Machiavelli, Niccolo *The Prince*, trs Luigi Ricci, rev. E.R.P. Vincent, Oxford University Press (World's Classics), Oxford 1935, reprinted 1949

7 Educational administration

7.1 A director's assessment
Michael Stoten

Then

When I began my working life as a teacher I doubt whether any of us in education ever gave a thought to accountability — although I suspect many practised it through a willingness to learn and a wish to do the best possible job. There were no obvious structures and certainly no considered processes of accountability other than the time-honoured examination results. Even these were never published in the form which is being promoted today. One of my more cynical colleagues at the time commented to me that 'good results reflected on the school, bad ones on the kids'.

The kind of organisation we had then made it possible to perpetuate that approach. Other than at the annual open evening (very one-sided affairs) we never saw parents, reports were short and standard, and I do not recall reviewing my progress at all with anyone during my years at the school. Nor at least in the early years did I set objectives or have them set for me: the syllabus was supposed to do that. I never saw an Inspector (HM or otherwise) or adviser during my entire teaching career except one who interviewed me for an internal promotion — which I did not get.

Yet it was a good school — well established, demonstrating a smooth transition from grammar to comprehensive, highly thought of by parents and with staff who knew what they were doing and appeared to me highly competent. Perhaps they were never really tested in difficult circumstances. As teachers we had power: I suspect we took accountability for granted, and maybe that was not such a bad thing. Perhaps it came naturally — more about that later.

When I entered the bureaucracy the manifestation of power widened. Now it wasn't just over pupils, but over staff and parents too. Whilst I hope it was not dangerous giving me all this, it might have been, and after two or three years we began to see a shift which, rightly in my view, made things more difficult.

The best example of many which I could give was concerned with school admissions. As an assistant education officer I had the power to decide, within the not-too-convincingly written policies of the LEA, whether a child could or could not attend a particular school. I saw many parents, some of whom went away satisfied; but others did not. All went bureaucratically well until some dissatisfied parents began to appeal to the Secretary of State. (Although I always told them they could they never had until then.) Whilst he did not direct a change as a rule, he evidently felt a need to act on what was a growing number of parents appealing to him against the decisions of their particular LEAs. The outcome of that was a hefty chapter in the Education Act 1980 which introduced much tighter controls on us on the one hand and greater flexibility and choice for parents on the other. I surprised myself by embracing the new approach, mainly I suspect because it codified and provided me with a framework in which to work, and which, by an appeals process, confirmed or amended my decision. I was offered continuing responsibility, lost power, and gained an accountability which made me look very carefully at the decisions I was given to make. I actually felt more confident and protected in what I was doing and I hope parents got a good deal from me too. This one example was reflected throughout LEAs' responsibilities, and the new(ish) approach was a modest foretaste of what was to come. It is also interesting that the Secretary of State of the time accepted local responsibility without central direction — provided the machinery was in place to protect the interests of individuals.

Now

We clearly have major changes since those first gentle stirrings of reform, and more are to come. At the time of writing the shelf-life of a chief officer is becoming discernibly shorter. As LEAs we have not only seen a shift in power but also a shift in responsibility down to an individual (school or person) level. Curiously this has manifested itself at a time when the accountability of LEAs has never been greater and the machinery to ensure accountability has never been more thorough. This accountability takes many forms; for example:

Personal satisfaction. The rights of individuals correctly take precedence over the convenience of the bureaucracy. We have to see that those rights are protected: we may also have to remind individuals that with rights come responsibilities — and accountabilities of their own.

Value for money, through information and to a significant extent control.

Performance monitoring, through indicators both quantitative and qualitative, and consistent review.

These are the kinds of accountability indicators which LEAs have introduced and have largely accepted as being useful and offer both performance measures and comfort. Performance monitoring is a little like visiting the dentist: never pleasant but if everything is fine, it is good to know. If it is not, it is as well to know so that matters can be put right.

The last 10 years have made explicit the view that those of us who have responsibility or power must be seen to use it wisely and for the benefit of those we serve, who may be more vulnerable than ourselves. To do that successfully must give enormous satisfaction: what we need is the confidence to carry it through.

As individuals we all want an educative process which brings out the best in children and meets their aspirations as well as ours. As a chief officer I want the accountabilities of all those concerned with education — pupils, parents, teachers, governors, LEA and government — to reflect responsibilities. There is no real accountability if responsibility lies elsewhere. I welcome putting responsibility where decision-making should be. But this requires circumstances in which people can operate and in which those acquiring responsibility recognise that their performance must come under scrutiny. It also requires that they have the mental toughness to deal with the reality of being in the hot seat. My job as chief officer is to ensure the hot seat merely stays warm. This requires mental toughness on their part and the skill to make the pressures tolerable on mine.

Partnership or hierarchy?

It is not difficult to construct a hierarchical organisation in which A is accountable to B who is accountable to C and so on. That this will work is not in dispute providing:

only one organisation is involved
the boundaries are carefully drawn
the weakest relationship in the chain doesn't break.

Education is not like that: the structures, whilst individually discrete are, in the general scheme of things, amorphous. There are not the direct channels of command and control which exist in, for example, a commercial organisation. Indeed the various interests, while having the same philosophical objectives so far as children are concerned, may actually be very different in character, and there may be major tensions between them.

The implication of this is that, to be effective, the main participants have to find sensible ways of working together — in such a manner that overall goals are stated and understood, who does what is clearly defined and the responsibility for action, decision-making and monitoring is well established. There are three conditions for this to be achieved.

Lines of communication must be short and units of management relatively small. There is nothing more frustrating than to go through tier upon tier of non-active personnel before action is achieved. This raises interesting points on how grant-maintained schools will be overseen in the future as well as for the management processes of larger local authorities.

No-one can take responsibility without having recourse to information and the means to use that information. The way it is used can improve or destroy an organisation.

No organisation will survive without trust. It appears to many of us in the education service that over the past 10 or so years there has been a factionalising of the various participants of the service — to lay blame for shortcomings and to feed discontent in simplistic and usually misinformed ways. That is a pity: there are few people in any area of education, whether providers or receivers, who do not see the value of working closely together. To generalise individual instances of breakdown does a disservice to the majority who recognise shared values and value each other. If we cannot learn to trust one another, then, in an atmosphere of distrust, the positive aspects of accountability will never surface.

If the various participants understand their place in the scheme of things and the limits of their influence and responsibility, there can be a constructive process of accountability.

Providers — government and local authorities

It used to be said that education was 'a national system locally administered'. For 30 years after 1944, whilst government contributed very significantly in financial terms, local influence on the curriculum and character of the service grew and that of central government on the delivery of the service declined. The 1980s saw a shift to greater government direction, culminating in the 1988 Act. The then rate support grant declined but funds became earmarked for national initiatives — in-service training, specific projects and now grant-maintained schools.

There is a move to regard LEAs now as 'enablers' or 'commissioners', but at the time of writing they are still providers to schools in terms of money, expertise, and — critically — evaluation of performance (though a shift of responsibility is foreshadowed here).

In terms of accountability the government is regarded as being susceptible at the ballot box every four or five years. For the LEA the position is somewhat different. Even in London, where local elections take place only every four years, there is real continuing local influence and pressure to change. Elected council members are subject to this constantly through their parties and constituents and provide a much closer accountability than government. It will be interesting to see what machinery government puts in place to manage those establishments currently and potentially funded directly by it if and as grant-maintained schools multiply. If LEAs survive, most of their non-statutory functions will be a matter of choice for schools who will be acting as customers rather than simply receiving a service.

They will call the tune because they will be paying the piper. I am reasonably comfortable with that. My view — and my LEA is working towards this practical approach — is that to be properly accountable we must provide a service which schools want, need, and are prepared to pay for. If we cannot, then someone else should. My only reservation is that, if we are going to compete the competition must be fair for us too: we should compete more widely than in our own area — just as our competitors will.

Given that LEAs are clearly accountable, we hope that government will understand and acknowledge that we have a proper and valuable role. We can put into place ways by which we account for what we do and, in present statutory terms, we can ensure that the accountability of schools is clearly and sensitively tested through our duty to evaluate and monitor performance.

Deliverers — governors and teachers

I have touched previously, if lightly, on the accountability of teachers. Moves to introduce formal accountability are well known, and in my authority are well advanced. The 'secret garden' is a secret no more. That is as it should be, but I worry that a climate of fear might be built up. A teacher's accountability must be seen to enhance professional quality and capacity. Most teachers have embraced the notion of local responsibility, and they will also face their own accountability. They will do so best through structured arrangements and in a climate of trust.

It is the governors whose role should be dramatically changing. They now have real power and responsibility — perhaps more than many envisaged or even wanted — and they can be great agents for good. Most of our governors are seizing the advantages of new freedoms, but it is now their performance (rather than that of the aunt sally LEA) which will come under scrutiny — both from parents and

LEA itself. I believe for example that governors will need to be more penetrative in carrying out their duties as they affect the curriculum.

Receivers — parents and children

It could be argued that parents are among the 'deliverers': certainly they are active participants. As guardians of their children's future, however, they are receivers. Over the last few years the participation of parents in education has been promoted at a structural level — on governing bodies, on consultative committees and through freedom of choice. The question is how far most parents have actually become involved directly in children's education. Probably more than previously, I suspect, but still not enough. Handing over more responsibility to parents will not in itself improve education, but it might naturally increase accountability in others. But what about the accountability of parents themselves which accompanies their rights? The parents that I know agree that they have a duty to ensure that their children do not foul either their own prospects or those of other children; to support the school in its aims and objectives providing these are understood and acceptable; to take an interest and where possible an active part in their children's learning. That kind of acceptance, perhaps even formally articulated in an agreement, can be enormously productive. This can be extended to pupils too whose interests and rights are, correctly, jealously protected but who also have responsibilities and accountabilities which match those of their parents, whether concerned with their academic performance, behaviour, or anything which affects the school and community. They too are accountable for the product of their actions. In my authority we have said we will not require a school to admit a pupil whose past record, after every effort by others, makes us sure that he or she will have a detrimental effect on the school and its teaching. This may be doubtful under one law but defensible, I believe, under others, which means that the onus is then on us to protect the rights of that individual in some other way.

These providers, deliverers and receivers are the partners in education. They need to work together. Accountabilities are one way of creating that framework of mutual respect and support through which comes confidence. What then, might be the machinery of accountability?.

The machinery of accountability

For accountability to have meaning it must have certain characteristics:

it must be understood by the parties concerned; achievable for them and acceptable to them; it must have an end product which can be judged.

Its machinery will come in many forms, all related and relevant to one another, however loosely. The following suggests a machinery of accountability for a director of education or chief education officer.

Self-accountability

This may seem a curious concept, but in my view self-accountability is the most important of all and it can certainly be the most powerful agent for change and the achievement of confidence. It is the means of challenging our own performance — of asking ourselves how well we have done, what needs to be done next and how we are affecting others. In essence we are judging the quality of our own performance, and external moderation, whilst important, is secondary to internal assessment. It is a move from the 'customer-care' ideal, of necessity largely imposed from outside, towards personal quality management where everything we do is naturally undertaken to the best of our ability. Such a strategy is not easy to achieve and requires great self-discipline. It may also from time to time be helpful to have the mutual support of others. The outcome however can be quite astonishing. In our education department we have been introducing quality management. One consequence of this is that I see all letters of complaint about departmental performance. I find that very hard, because I believe they reflect on me and I do not like reading them. But by doing so I can establish my own self-accountability; importantly, do something about it, and establish an accountability link with others concerned. By chasing up, seeking out and where necessary putting right, performance is improved generally in the department and I am in this respect directly fulfilling my overall responsibility to the public. It also means that colleagues are not isolated — whether right or wrong they do not stand alone.

Communication

Other forms of accountability involve other people. With them lines of communication must be short and effective: people have to be talking about the same things in similar language. A good example of this in my local authority concerns communicating with parents. We set up two groups of parents — one for those of children with special educational needs, who previously had been little involved, and the other with representative parents, some dozen of them, from mainstream schools. We were looking not just for talk or information but for genuine working groups. The special needs group has worked as

well, if not better, than we could have hoped. Meetings are productive, the issues clear and there is a capacity and willingness to work to
solutions.

The other group has been less successful, because our separate
objectives, as opposed to the agreed overall objectives, have become
somewhat different. The parents, not unreasonably, want to understand and be involved in strategic LEA issues. My purpose has been
much more directed to operational matters such as homework and
discipline. Having recognised that we were drifting we have been
sufficiently close to work up a common approach which I expect can
satisfy both our requirements. Communication must be not only
rapid and effective, but also open to review.

Leadership

Again this may be thought a curious inclusion in the machinery of
accountability, but the success of an organisation, even such an
allegedly democratic one as an LEA, can be determined by the
quality of leadership. Leadership qualities are largely common to all
spheres of the service: outside the purely professional competencies
there are 'management' attributes which are the same for CEOs,
heads, team leaders, chairmen of governors and so on. In an exercise
by external consultants on headteacher competencies, most were
found to be related to style and dealing with people.

The critical difference was between leadership, which was highly
participative yet recognised where the buck stopped, and dictator-
ship — which was the adoption, by decree, of personal ambition.
Much of our management development recently has been conceived
with people taking responsibility in such a way that others are, as far
as possible, taken along with them. It is at the point of final decision-
making by individuals within their own remit which determines
good leadership and good management. A sound understanding of
the boundaries of responsibility and the obligation towards people
within them produces convincing accountability.

Responsibility at the point of action

We have subscribed cheerfully to the devolvement of responsibility
to individual schools and governing bodies. My LEA has accepted
the principle that those things which can be devolved should be, and I
expect to see a substantial part of the present education department in
the future very much as a contractor to the school as client. The level
of service and choice of contractor is the school's. The accountability
here is two-fold. First, I am accountable to schools for the services
the LEA provides: poor service, no deal. Second, schools are accountable for the decisions they make on whether to accept LEA
services, or someone else's, or simply spend the money differently.

It is my purpose to ensure that schools and governing bodies are sufficiently trained and confident to make good, defensible decisions. We are thus making gentle, but thorough, pace in devolution, a pace schools find manageable.

Objective setting

We manage accountability for both individuals and, to an extent, establishments, by objective setting. This is nothing new. Management by objectives (MBO) was fashionable in the early '80s but still works in the form of appraisal, performance monitoring and performance review. We use it throughout the council — for performance monitoring of officers and committees, for appraisal of teachers, for performance-related remuneration for senior officers, heads and deputies.

We ask where are we? — where do we want to be? — how do we get there? — how do we know we have arrived?

It is a process which gives people confidence. At an individual level it forms a part, and only a part, of professional development. All of our staff will have individual career development plans: objective setting, personal to and agreed by them, plays a major role. Again, it is important that the process is underpinned by support. It is no good saying to someone, 'You have not achieved this objective' without having the means to put matters right. When those are in place the sense of individual confidence can be quite startling even after a less than brilliant performance.

Performance indicators

Performance indicators can form a useful part of objective setting and appraisal at any level, from organisation to individual. Unfortunately much that has been written about performance indicators has been highly politicised — the argument for example of whether to publish raw or weighted examination results has caused a lot of recent grief. Properly used, performance indicators do have a real value but we have to distinguish different types and link them together. There are three types: input indicators are concerned with the circumstances in which schools or individuals find themselves (an example might be social disadvantage); output indicators are largely concerned with pupil performance (for example exam results); and process indicators are about how people operate within a particular set of circumstances to produce a particular level of result.

Taken separately they may not be very convincing (I remember a councillor telling a conference that his was the most efficient LEA in the country because it had the highest pupil-teacher ratio. It also had the worst exam results.) Taken sensibly and putting the relevant information from the three types together, performance indicators can give good clues about how well we are doing. I value them in that form and so too do my members and, I believe, staff and governors.

Inspection

Inspection can and should be a major public determinant of how well a school and its staff are performing — how well they are discharging their responsibilities. Much of an inspection, whilst relying on quantitative information to an extent, will be based on objective professional judgement. Where an inspection of the more penetrative kind may not be well established in an LEA, there is scope for tension.

That our inspections have worked well is a tribute both to the staff in schools and to the inspectors. We inspect, and inspect fully, but we prepare the ground in advance. We also follow up, both by offering support in making changes and ensuring, so far as our powers permit, that changes are made. I was asked, elsewhere, to form a 'hit squad' of inspectors; I declined and believe I was right to do so. I think we achieve greater commitment and respect by seeing the process through as part of the LEA's accountability to its staff and students. The outcome is not always comfortable, for the LEA, governors or staff, but it can be productive in a climate of understanding and trust.

Conclusion

These, then, are the structures of accountability. What matters is that the process works, and works for people. The object is high quality in schools, and there are many ways of achieving this. There is a delicate balance to be maintained between the partners in the service if education is to account for itself with confidence.

7.2 Managing change
Gordon Lister

The hallmark of every successful organisation is its capacity to manage change, using all its resources and committing all its personnel to a positive outcome. Of course education has experienced rapid change, but so has the rest of the public sector, not to mention the private sector which is riding out a recession. That pace of change will continue. The government has required competition and contracting out of local government services, seeing the local authority as enabling rather than providing services. There has been a much-needed exhortation to focus on the consumers and clients of our services. It has also been a decade of financial restraint, with local authorities having to re-think provision and re-order priorities. These changes have put a premium on management skills, not our traditional strength in either local government or education.

The future is not going to be very different. Our accountability to the public will be restated and sharpened through the *Citizen's Charter* which had been promised by Labour as well as the Conservatives. The Training and Enterprise Councils will be developed. More services will be contracted out.

Resources will not increase significantly.

Most importantly, there will be a far-reaching review of the functions, structure and funding of local government. Critical to that review will be a decision on how education is to be managed into the next century.

There are, I believe, two main possibilities for education in the medium term.

The first would derive from a continuation, and indeed acceleration, of current government policy on education and training. Grant-maintained status would become the driving force of education reform, and key features would include:

- all secondary schools to be grant-maintained — nationally funded by a funding council;
- more than 10 per cent of primary schools grant-maintained;
- all further education colleges under the FE funding council;
- an enhanced role for the TECs;
- a nationalised, arms-length quality assurance function through a restructured HMI.

The local authority — if it continued — would be left with residual responsibility for managing non-grant-maintained primary schools; special schools; a minimal range of statutory services.

The second possibility would be in a climate more favourable to local authorities but with many significant changes still on the agenda. Local management would be the motor of education reform. Key features would include:

- no further grant-maintained schools — existing grant-maintained schools either returned to the local authority or left as free-standing institutions;
- further development of local management;
- the long-term prospect of single-tier most-purpose authorities based neither on existing districts nor on shires;
- possibly regional government with responsibility for strategic planning, economic development, highways, further and work-related education.

Both possibilities imply a different role for local authorities, and the issue in both will be the value the local authority adds to the education service. Our future in the administrative part of local government should and will depend on this.

Added value is simply another way of defining local authority accountability, and I wish to relate it to my own authority and the response that we are making. Cambridgeshire perhaps has an advantage in that it pioneered the original concept and practice of local management in schools and colleges. It was based on a philosophy shared by all three of the political groups on the council that local management is about enhancing the quality of education through genuine decision-making by headteachers and governors on all matters that affect their schools or colleges. We may not have liked some of the expression of this in the Education Reform Act 1988, but it was not imposed on us. We believe passionately that local management and community involvement in the service is one of the most positive and exciting developments of democracy in this century.

Once you have embarked on a policy which involves a fundamental shift of responsibility you do have to re-define accountabilities and accept that this is not a once-and-for-all process. So three years ago, as a result of the changes in relationships and responsibilities brought about by local management in education, in social services and transport, we decided to review in a radical way the role of the council and its support services.

We recognised that, once you have devolved responsibility to a local level, then, for example, the Education Committee has to change — it cannot second-guess the decisions made by each school.

We have, therefore, streamlined our decision-making. We have swept away education subcommittees. The education committee itself has been drastically reduced in size and it meets no more than half-a-dozen times each year with agendas almost entirely concerned with strategic and quality issues. Members recognise that being a governor of their local school is as important as sitting on the education committee.

In Cambridgeshire, therefore, we have re-defined the account-abilities of the LEA as being about:

Planning: providing or reducing provision in relation to demographic changes and parental choice, and deciding on the most effective pattern of school and college organisation;

Quality control and improvement of standards: information to parents and students about all the choices of establishments and courses available to them;

Funding of locally-determined services like community education, nursery education and certain kinds of home-to-school transport which, at a cost, add value to the basic level of education.

As far as support services are concerned, we have removed area offices and started with a 'blank sheet' proposition that the LEA shall be that which headteachers and governors will collectively invent. We have accepted that the LEA does not have a right to exist unless we can demonstrate our worth. We are committed to a 'buyer-driven approach' for all support services. This means that resources for financial or personnel advice are now being transferred, without conditions, to heads and governors who will then choose whether or not they want to spend money on these services and, if so, which suppliers they want to engage. This change is being applied to all council services, not just education.

This transformation in traditional accountabilities has been mirrored by changes in the roles and responsibilities of governors and headteachers. There is now a proper demand from our heads and governors for full participation in the decision-making of the LEA. They are already 'buyers' of support services: quite rightly they are now assuming a greater role as 'stakeholders'. Cambridgeshire governors want to know about and influence not just how their own school budgets are spent, but how they are generated, how they compare with others, how standard spending assessments are calculated, what special factors affect Cambridgeshire and so on. This is to be welcomed. Schools do not stand in isolation. They must work with their funding bodies and their neighbouring establishments. They must, therefore, be consulted about many matters relating to budget generation, budget distribution and service planning. This will include involvement in decisions on services which work across institutional arrangements. We are therefore creating a chair of governors' forum to face the political system.

More controversially, we are developing a response which reflects the pivotal responsibility of heads as prime managers of an integrated service and, in particular, their contribution to the strategic management of the LEA in a new contractual relationship. Head-teachers and principals are now discharging new accountabilities to their governors and the LEA and it is right that they be appraised and rewarded appropriately. We believe that it is valuable and necessary to define unequivocally the tripartite relationship between the head, governing body and LEA. An integral part of this approach will be a full-scale performance appraisal of the head carried out each year by the director of education and the chair of governors.

What of the future? Shall we have been hoist by our own petard in Cambridgeshire? I hope not. Just as it is the responsibility of the education service to give children confidence in themselves and to equip them to fulfil their potential, I believe that it is a prime responsibility of every LEA to encourage and support all of its institutions to become truly self-managing. There are cynics who say to us 'all you are doing is making it easier for schools to opt out'. If schools can get to that stage in management maturity, the obvious next step is to leave the LEA altogether. That is what the Secretary of State also asserts — that the natural next step from LMS is GMS.

That argument could not be more wrong. It is not to say that GMS is not to be taken seriously. On the contrary, everyone should be constantly alert to what is being offered, in the short and the long term. For all I know, there could be a White Paper next week setting a timetable by which schools had to go GMS, or the funding regime could be such that no responsible governing body could afford not to give GMS very careful consideration. It is still important to consider the long-term consequences, including the implicit demise of local democratic government for education.

If it were forced, however, I would be pleased that Cambridgeshire schools were strong, experienced and robust enough to make the best of it.

I am not hostile to the heads' and governing bodies' giving close consideration to GMS. My hostility is to the argument that what we are doing leads to a situation where all schools in Cambridgeshire will naturally and logically choose GMS, assuming that this choice remains a realistic one. The prevailing view amongst our heads is exactly the opposite.

Most of us start from the premise that it is important to plan public education for all children and all needs. That is the duty laid on LEAs by the 1944 and 1981 Education Acts. The market cannot be relied on necessarily to provide places appropriate to every pupil's needs. It can and maybe should be relied on to provide some support services of various kinds to schools. But it cannot guarantee local places, of an appropriate quality, for all children. It cannot guarantee fairness in admission arrangements. It cannot of itself guarantee quality.

I have followed with great interest the professional and managerial debate in our county about the devolution of, for example, the music or school library service.

What has actually been said by heads and governors of secondary schools is, 'yes, we shall be buyers if that means the service will be more responsive to our needs — but not on a crude commercial basis where unthinking, unshared individual decisions lead in aggregate to an adverse impact on the overall quality of service for all other buyers'. That is why the term stakeholder is so much better than buyer. 'Stakeholder' includes all the opportunities and responsibilities of the buying function, but puts that buying function in a context of collaborative shared responsibility for all schools.

The argument grows very quickly from that point. Heads are saying that they want to be stakeholders in a particular kind of LEA: one that holds values about individual entitlement, access for all pupils, community education, continuity between different stages in education; one that can agree collectively about priorities for, perhaps, new approaches to pupils with disruptive behaviour, or particular aspects of teacher training, or provision for environmental and residential education.

These things have to be decided as far as possible collectively and professionally. Other things have to be given up for them. In effect, schools choose to yield freedom and resources that they could otherwise have because that is the way they see the greater good being secured. That is the natural next step to LMS, not GMS. Opting in to the LEA, opting in to Cambridgeshire, is not a shopping decision — that you choose to buy from the LEA because you like its products. Opting in to Cambridgeshire comes about when you see yourselves and operate as stakeholders with shared responsibility for all pupils. I also believe that this should be constitutionally underwritten by a democratically elected local authority.

I would not claim that we have got it right or that all our changes are the right ones, but I do strongly believe that if local government loses its responsibility for education it will be because of those who have dragged their feet rather than those who have sought to initiate and manage change with enthusiasm.

8 Policy and performance

8.1 Have a good journey

Duncan McReddie and Jack Morrish

Our view of accountability in education is that of local politicians directly involved in the development of policy and its implementation. That does not mean that our sole concern is with political outcomes, even though we number among our accountabilities that which we owe to our respective electorates — and to our local political parties, through which our somewhat awesome responsibilities were thrust upon us. We can rightly be called to account by the voters and by our political peers. Many of our other areas of accountability are shared with the other 'partners' in the complicated network which develops the policies and which shapes the practices; but our primary accountability is to the children and students in our schools and colleges and those within the extended continuum of education.

It was a politician who reminded his readers that 'theory without practice is sterile, and practice without theory is blind'. Theory is largely the embodiment of accumulated practice. The same is true of policy and practice, and a rigid dividing line between them is destructive. We do not ensure the achievement of our objectives by separating them, by insisting either that the practitioners have no role in policy-making or that policy-makers are unconcerned with implementation. The confidence that ensures good practice and the attainment of objectives is derived in large measure from the commitment of all concerned to policies to which they have contributed and which they feel they 'own'. We take as our starting point this inextricability of policy and practice.

The framework and nature of policy

It would be facile and inaccurate to see policy only in terms of major strategic objectives. Even with the over-centralisation of decision-making in so many important aspects of education, with so much power vested in the Secretary of State through the Education Reform Act 1988, there are levels of policy which are the responsibility of either local education authorities or the schools and colleges. As chairs of education committees we have become only too well aware that the policy responsibilities of LEAs have significantly decreased, whilst those of schools and colleges have increased. Unfortunately the redistribution of power has not always matched the new pattern of responsibility. This is particularly so in respect of resources which are even more at the mercy of central government than hitherto. All participants in education's jigsaw of accountabilities will gain in confidence to the extent that they gain clarity about the boundaries of their responsibilities and the extent of their powers; this is equally true of both policy and practice. It is not good enough to say that the LEA, through its education committee, has the job of deciding overall policy; that the governing body sets the aims and objectives for its school; that it is for the director of education or CEO and the headteacher, with their respective staffs, to get on with the detailed planning and day-to-day managing. Just as unhelpful is the familiar declaration that governors govern whilst headteachers manage. Such formulations are imprecise, unclear and in some respects inaccurate. They risk duplication, dereliction and unnecessary conflict.

The making of policy

Since the Education Act of 1986 and 1988 central government has heavily exercised its wider policy-making powers: the National Curriculum is rapidly taking shape; the constitution and powers of governing bodies have been transformed; overall local government expenditure has been circumscribed, with an inevitable reduction in real expenditure on education in almost every authority area (irrespective of its political complexion); the distribution of funds between schools is formula-driven on a basis subject to Whitehall veto; higher education has been largely removed from the LEA sphere of influence and further education is about to go the same way; the role of LEAs in the determination of teachers' pay and conditions has been marginalised; schools have been enabled to 'opt out' of the LEA and more recently have been encouraged (even bribed) to do so; parents have been asked to accept a crude consumerist view about their children's education.

In spite of this planned erosion of the role of the LEA, many important areas of policy still remain for local determination and it might be helpful to describe and analyse how one of our authorities, Cleveland, went about the task in the wake of the county council elections.

In May, 1989, the policies contained in the majority party's manifesto — on which the Cleveland County Labour Party had fought and won that election — were incorporated into the education committee minutes, and were used as the basis for five guiding principles which would shape the way in which the service would run. They appeared in a 'mission statement', the central message of which was partnership based on contribution, coherence, communication, community and commitment. That statement concluded with a series of 'action points' which declared that the LEA would:

- support the effectiveness of teachers, lecturers and other staff in schools, colleges and other education institutions;
- determine the appropriate level of resources to meet the needs of institutions and organisations within the service;
- secure the distribution of resources so far as to meet all needs, with an emphasis on those disadvantaged groups;
- ensure that county council and external funds are directed in the most effective way;
- foster an atmosphere where criticism is reasoned and positive and where change can take place without dislocation;
- provide an accountable service with monitoring, reporting and complaints procedures which are open and purposeful.

(We are tempted to reflect that this statement was an earlier, shorter, and perhaps better version of what is now described as a parents' charter!)

A 'shopping list' of specific improvements was deliberately avoided since this was deemed a dangerous course in the current education climate where the only certainty was uncertainty. Limited immediate objectives were thought more appropriate to short-term year-to-year planning.

Once established, this policy became the basis for staff training and a guide for departmental action. It was also the starting-point for a series of seminars involving all staff from the chief executive and the education officer to the most junior administrative and clerical personnel. Their views were elicited and in particular they were invited to consider their own role and what the policy would require of them. This process revealed significant differences in perceived priorities and it was decided that a series of officer working parties should be charged with the job of producing a new departmental ethos leading to new working methods. In turn, this led to the production of a departmental brochure available to all parents and governors, and to the incorporation of the new ethos into the job descriptions of both senior and junior officers.

These tasks were tackled with enthusiasm by the officers and the successful outcome owes much to the recognition that their own 'instinctive' working methods were being incorporated and codified and that the statement provided a basis for thinking and planning.

A variation on this theme of policy development is exemplified by the experience in Northamptonshire during the administration of 1981-85. As in Cleveland, the starting point was the election manifesto of the majority party. It was presented to the education officer to plan a phased implementation with a request for advice and for officers' views on practicality and priorities. The 'professionals' were also invited to propose additional (rather than alternative) projects derived from internal experience.

Work was immediately put in hand for an improvement in the pupil-teacher ratio, a significant increase in capitation expenditure, a decrease in the price of school meals, the rapid development of additional nursery units and other measures for which there was known support among teachers and in the wider community.

Policy proposals which required more fundamental examination and detailed formulation were remitted to joint working parties comprising officers, members from all political groupings, staff representatives and parents, many of whom also served on governing bodies. These proposals included a fundamental review of the curriculum, in which every teacher participated through in-service training, and the development of records of achievement. Instruments and articles of school governance were rewritten, building on earlier reforms, and which together led to the introduction of most of the Taylor Committee recommendations well in advance of the 1986 Act.

There are lessons to be learnt from these two briefly described examples. It is recognised that politicians are not the only people involved in policy determination, even though they are rightly the final arbiters on major matters, particularly (but not solely) where additional or redeployed resources are involved; but those same politicians ignore at their peril the advice, professional expertise and accumulated experience of all other partners. There is a clear need for early input from the 'professionals' and from the many legitimate interest groups (sometimes misnamed 'pressure groups') such as those representing various ethnic communities and those concerned with children with special needs. It is equally important that the trade unions, parents' organisations and, above all, governing bodies should be drawn into the process.

Those with power at higher and intermediate levels should not ignore others who are affected by the use of that power; and this is particularly true where decisions taken at one level create insuperable constraints for those at a 'lower' level. This cascade effect of policy-making, which is acute in the field of education, requires those at lower levels to press for changes in higher-level decisions where their own ability to deliver is impaired. Such is the logic of accountability, where each decision-maker must take account of the interests of other decision-makers and also of the decision implementors.

What we are here arguing is that good practice is fostered by securing, wherever possible, a consensus in policy determination. Such a process enables each interdependent partner to understand the constraints as well as the priorities of others. It ensures a 'bottom-up' element to accompany the normal top-down approach and implies a duty as well as a right to contribute constructively and at times forcibly.

There is a further implication. If the political manifesto is to be a credible basic policy document commanding loyal support for post-election implementation, there must be an acceptable mechanism for 'bottom-up' input, involving rank-and-file members of the party as well as parents, students and others employed in education. There should be an early dialogue with senior education officers, within improved and agreed conventions applicable to all political parties, to explore what can be achieved and afforded. This latter involvement does not imply handing the policy role to the professionals, but it does prevent their implied exclusion from policy-making and the danger of losing their enthusiastic commitment. And in any case the art of the politician in achieving the possible includes the flair for extending the boundaries of the possible and the affordable.

Before moving from policy to practice we need to ensure that the overarching aims, values and ethos of the mission statement are supplemented by a sufficiently detailed development plan with short-term and medium-term targets. This will mirror the process enjoined upon governing bodies and will also provide a clear background for the formulation of school development plans. The resulting action plan will not be unalterable: it will be tested and regularly evaluated in the light of ensuing practice. Both policy and practice will be enriched by dynamic inter-action.

Practice — the art of implementation

Although no self-respecting LEA will cease to urge central government to modify those policies and regulations that appear to obstruct good local provision, immediate practice will be constrained within statutory obligations and the imposed financial straitjacket. The LEA development plan and the annual budget for the education service will provide the starting-point for implementation at school level. This brings us to the all-important relationship between LEA, headteacher and governing body, where practice is changing so rapidly, where variation between schools and between LEAs is considerable, and where all participants are having to learn fast. As before, we have chosen to proceed from real examples, particularly of governing bodies and the way in which the LEA works with its schools. The approach can be through conflict, confrontation and competition; or through co-operation. Cleveland chose co-operation, in line with its mission statement.

By way of background it can be recalled that a previous chair of the education committee, Peter Fulton, was the member of the 1977

Commission of Enquiry that led to the Taylor Report who issued a minority report. He believed that only the elected members of the LEA were truly accountable and he accordingly withheld support for some of the report's main recommendations on the ground that they would devolve power 'to a non-elected and unrepresentative body/authority without any accountability'. These views reflected the failure of many governors to accept the responsibilities given to them 33 years earlier by the Education Act, 1944. Even today some councillors voice similar criticisms, overlooking the culpability of the many LEAs that neither encouraged nor trained governors to play their intended part.

This negative view of governors has largely dissipated in the aftermath of the 1986 Act which so markedly altered the composition of many governing bodies and extended and more clearly defined their powers and duties. Cleveland and most other LEAs now recognise their duty to train and educate governors to discharge those responsibilities, to understand their corporate accountability and to exercise this in concert with the other accountable parties.

The Education Reform Act 1988 has led many LEAs to reappraise their own role and their relationship with school governors. The need is seen to move away from that paternalism wherein the voters were expected to leave matters to the elected councillors and to be quietly grateful. Reluctant authorities are now aware that governors have powers as well as duties and might even use them.

This recognition and the other provisions of the 1988 Act have shifted the balance of the relations between LEAs and governing bodies. There are many changes that could lead to unhelpful and unhealthy competition between schools and to the destruction of trust between them and the LEA: the opportunity for schools to 'opt out' and secure grant-maintained status; the adverse effect of such opting out on the budgets of other schools; the effect of open enrolment, particularly where schools are adjacent in larger urban areas; the shortage of teachers and the temptation facing governors to use the considerable discretion now available to enhance the salaries of heads and other teachers—in short, the worst aspects of market rivalry where the weakest, or those perceived (often wrongly) to be the weakest, could go to the wall.

Cleveland's answer was to require officers of the LEA, with the unobtrusive involvement of members, to respond sensitively to the needs of the schools. The members gave priority to effective two-way communication with governors, firstly to convince them that whilst the education committee shared the concerns of the particular school it was necessary to bear also in mind the needs of the other 262 schools when tailoring expenditure and formulating policies; secondly and perhaps even more importantly, to meet the problems which face governors and to identify with their aspirations for the future.

The framework devised for this essential interchange was a liaison subcommittee comprising eight members of the education committee — five from the controlling Labour group and three covering the two minority groups. It included the chairs and vice-chairs of the education committee and the major subcommittees. Meetings are held termly with area forums to which the chair and vice-chair of each governing body are invited; they are held at six or seven locations and at different times of the day in order to maximise participation. The agenda comprises those matters about which the LEA wishes to inform governors and those which governors wish to discuss; the latter are often identified at the separate termly meetings between the authority and chair or vice-chairs of governing bodies. The liaison subcommittee receives a report on each round of meetings and submits the report to the full education committee, with recommendations where appropriate. This model was devised for consultation and interaction and avoids the danger of domination by those from a particular area or phase of education.

We are aware that most authorities are moving on the same lines but with variations based on size, geography and other considerations. In several, including for example the London Borough of Hounslow, the education chair and vice-chairs join the director of education at meetings of headteachers and their governing body chairs. That same authority presents to each meeting of its education services subcommittee every resolution sent to the LEA by governing bodies and proposes draft responses.

In a growing number of authorities there are also emergent governor support groups, such as those in Hillingdon and parts of Northamptonshire, and this type of organisation, which is very much governor-initiated and led, might well provide governors with a more independent and co-ordinated input to the authority. But what is important in all this is that there is a rapid extension of machinery for consultation and co-operation and for the building of mutual understanding and confidence.

Quite naturally there are teething problems. Some elected members in particular are too voluble and at times defensive, feeling the need to justify their policies and actions. Some governors start with suspicion and might occasionally use the forum to attack policy rather than contribute to it. But even in these early stages there are far more positive indications that the mechanism is working. There has been little evidence of party political partisanship even though there has been a good deal of criticism of the Education Reform Act 1988. There is a greater understanding of local management and a recognition that it involves much more than budgets and balance sheets.

We have all become convinced that local management is here to stay and that it has positive value; there is, of course, room for improvement, and the random and arbitrary effects of formula funding must be remedied.

Neither local management alone nor the new machinery for co-operation guarantees accountability; but both encourage and facilitate it by contributing to the clarification of our respective roles and responsibilities and by creating a climate within which the essential understanding and mutual trust can flourish.

The accountabilities of the chair

This critical review of policy and practice is a form of accountability in itself. It also contributes to its definition and to the genesis of the necessary confidence which underpins its successful delivery.

We would now like to examine more closely the accountabilities of those who emerge as chairs of education committees. Inevitably this will be an extension of the role of the elected member who chooses to serve on the education committee. That very choice can be seen as the first act of accountability, since it involves acceptance of a shared responsibility to ensure good education. In making the choice we inherit the good fortune that those professionals with whom we shall be working also have a similar commitment, and frequently a level of enthusiasm well beyond that which is normal in other professions.

We need to ask three basic questions about accountability: for what? to whom? how? They cannot be answered in simplistic terms because of the nature of the venture in which we are engaged and the complicated machinery, statutory and otherwise, in which we are enmeshed.

The first must be answered in general terms, for we are politically accountable for the broad range of services provided by the education department; we cannot become prisoners of the needs of particular establishments nor slaves to a particular philosophy or methodology. That does not mean that the chair stands above the 'battle' of everyday delivery. It is often possible to perceive the need for policy adjustment by discovering what is happening in the field and by drawing lessons from that new knowledge. This process also assists those with responsibility at the 'chalkface' to meet better their individual accountability — and sometimes to ensure that they have the additional resources to make that possible.

To whom are we accountable? Certainly not to any single person or group, since the interests of one might be incompatible with those of another. For example, we cannot fall into the trap (as some politicians are prone to) of thinking that we must accede to every demand from each trade union. Nor can we always meet the request of one school if it means doing so at the expense of other schools. We shall at times have to accept responsibility for unpopular decisions. We should be forgiven if at times we imagine that we are responsible to the (Cleveland) *Evening Gazette* or to the (Northampton) *Chronicle and Echo*.

We can nevertheless identify some people and groups to whom we should be prepared to render an account. Foremost among these are the children, students and others for whom we provide the opportunity to learn; then there are the parents or guardians with whom we also have an implied contract. There is the wider community, including potential employers, that has a right to demand a good education service. In statutory matters we can certainly be called to account by central government. More locally, we have our electorate who made us councillors in the first place and our own party members and committees. Within the service we share a duty to the staff who provide the services and whom we expect to implement our policies. We accept the responsibilities we have to governing bodies since they are so dependent on our policies and the budgetary decisions we make. In the county council we must also share an accountability for corporate policy and to the corporate leadership.

The whole of this network of accountabilities would be ineffective unless it were backed by the most potent ingredient of all; the knowledge that we are accountable to our own consciences — which is so much more important than fleeting public acclaim or popularity. Reflecting on our own experiences as chairs of education committees we have gained a warm sense of fulfilment when planned improvements have come to fruition. We are equally aware of the frustration we have felt when other plans have been thwarted by lack of resources or by unhelpful central government dictat.

Perhaps the biggest single worry that we both have is that co-operation between schools and between the various providing partners will be replaced by mutual suspicion and divisive conflict. No child's future ought to be threatened by market-place competition between schools. Each school should have a vision of its future based upon hope, endeavour and consideration for others, rather than greed and a fear of losing out. The ethos of the school is quickly communicated to its children and students.

Moving to the 'how' question, we are bound to confess that there is even more scope for individuality of approach for committee chairs than there is for teachers in developing their style and methodology. For all of us there is the test of effectiveness and the achievement of declared and shared objectives measured over time. But it is equally important to know what is happening on the ground on a week-to-week basis through visits to schools and discussions with heads, teachers, governors, parents, children and students. We must also be approachable and ready to respond to criticism (which is more frequently constructive than destructive).

We have a particular responsibility at LEA level to assist governors to understand and exercise their responsibility; to ensure that they reach beyond the often mundane questions of day-to-day school management by gaining the confidence to become involved in the aims and objectives of the school, its curriculum and its development plan. Effective schools need effective governing bodies and an effective LEA working together as partners. We must learn to believe that we need each other.

The way forward

It is possible to summarise the approach that this article implies. If LEAs are allowed a future, and if we were privileged to play a part in that future, our guidelines would include the procedures listed below.

- consult widely with parents, professionals, special interest groups, and the wider community when preparing a political manifesto;
- ensure that the manifesto is a programme that can be realised within stretched resources;
- with the help of the professionals convert the programme into a LEA development plan;
- involve governing bodies in the preparation of the LEA plan and the dovetailing school development plans;
- set yearly objectives within a rolling medium-term programme;
- ensure ownership and understanding of such plans by those responsible for their delivery and by students and their parents;
- develop commitment through open two-way consultation;
- define the responsibility of each participating body and individual with precision;
- create simple machinery for regular review forums involving senior members, the chief education officer and his team, headteachers and governors;
- plan the training of governors so that there is maximum involvement in the joint processes described above;
- make sure that the political and professional leadership knows what is happening on the ground;
- ensure good communications but avoid mountainous paperwork;
- rely heavily on commonsense and good humour.

These are only broad ground rules which will take detailed shape at local level. For those embarking on this challenging but exciting course, the following recipe for a possible safe arrival is offered:

start the journey with a strategic map;
plan the destination — and the route;
seek allies and retain them;
make friends, not enemies;
look out for crossfire;
ensure adequate supplies;
carry a reliable loud-hailer;
recheck map reference at regular intervals;
use diversions to avoid road-blocks;
avoid the cul-de-sac;
laugh at the inevitable setbacks;
arrive before sundown;
have a good journey!

9 Educational purpose

9.1 Nightmares and visions in the 1990s

Robin Richardson

Chalkhill Primary School in north London nestles at the foot of gigantic tower blocks of flats, apparently overwhelmed by the grim and brutal buildings in which its pupils and their families live. The governors and staff at Chalkhill exercise their multiple accountabilities under the Education Reform Act in physical and social circumstances which most people elsewhere in the country would consider to be profoundly unpromising and profoundly inimical to a sense of confidence. Recently a child at the school wrote the following poem:

> I am rich and pure and full of fresh thoughts,
> Ready to take on the world.
> I'm full of action,
> Smart as anything,
> And full of quality.
> I am an egg ready to hatch.
> I bring with me life.[1]

The poem beautifully evokes one of the concepts with which this chapter and this book are concerned, that of confidence. The child is open to all the newness which the future has in store, and is marvellously confident of being able to shape personally the future's events and eventualities. As adults we are responsible for nurturing, protecting and resourcing such confidence, and for ensuring that it is warranted not only by children's own capabilities but also by the generosity and firmness of the world which we provide for them to grow up in, and which they will one day take over and run themselves.

The poem is also a reminder about multiple accountabilities. The governors and staff at Chalkhill are responsible not only upwards so to speak, to the government and its legislation, but also downwards to the children; not only backwards in time to the past and to cultural heritage but also forwards to the fabric of future society; and, in a social structure marked by severe disparities of wealth and power, they are accountable not only to the status quo but also to the communities and neighbourhoods which are most deprived and disadvantaged. How can the governors and staff at Chalkhill be and remain confident, as they wrestle with the myriad expectations and obligations placed upon them? And how can the governors and staff at thousands of other similar schools throughout Britain remain confident? These are the questions of this chapter.

The chapter has a three-part pattern. The first part is entitled 'The case for no confidence'. Its arguments will be presented in two different formats: first, luridly and melodramatically through a piece of perhaps heavy-handed satire, but then second quite soberly through a series of forecasts about the 1990s which will be shown, one day, to have been either accurate or false. The proposition, in both formats, is that it is very difficult indeed to be and to remain confident: nothing has improved in British society and in the education system during the last decade, and nothing is going to improve during the 1990s. On the contrary, there will be various worsenings and failures. We shall fail in our accountability to children and young people; in our accountability to the social fabric of future society; and in our accountability to the neighbourhoods and communities in present society which are most disadvantaged. The governors at Chalkhill, and at all other similar schools, don't stand a chance.

The second part of the chapter ought ideally to be entitled, and to constitute, 'The case for confidence'. It is perhaps significant that I cannot manage this, and that both the title and the theme for the second part are more modest. The title is 'The case against no confidence'. The third part of the chapter, emerging from the contradiction and clash between the first two parts, is entitled 'What then shall we do?'. This third part will offer a set of general principles to guide us in coping with the tensions between foreboding and confidence, and to guide the design of specific programmes, projects and activities.

The overall pattern is reminiscent of a law court. There will be two counsels, or advocates, opposing each other in adversarial fashion. Next, there will be the judge's summing-up. Finally, after the specialist parts have been concluded, it will be up to the jury — that is, in the present instance, the reader — to take the matter further. My task, as I play in turn the roles of the two advocates and of the judge, is to provide a resource for you, the jury. The nightmare, the critique and the summing-up are all offered for judgement.

The governors at Chalkhill have to take account not only of national policies but also those of their local authority, which happens to be the London Borough of Brent. It is relevant to mention that Brent has published a curriculum document, *Equality and Excellence*, whose opening sentence contains a vision of persons and of learning which is reminiscent of the optimism and confidence expressed in the child's poem, and of the poem's sense of boundless and unknowable possibilities:

All learners are of equal value, and have unlimited potential for development.[2]

It is from the value-position presented in *Equality and Excellence* as introduced and sketched lightly in its opening sentence, that this paper is written. In order to keep it in mind the paper will frequently quote from poems written about or by children and young people, recalling their life-worlds and their fears, and their stories and hopes. For the principle of downwards accountability to learners surely requires, as a simple matter of logic, that our search for confidence needs to be informed, inspired and challenged by the perceptions, accounts and experiences of children. One of our central mottoes may valuably and appropriately be therefore that remark of Froebel's in the 19th century: 'Attend to the child, the child will tell you what to do'.

Let us recall the world-view of a child. This poem is by Bill Allchin, a psychotherapist, and it is entitled *Little Girl to School*:

> Snowface unwarmed by
> redflamed hair and a woolly cap,
> feet stuck to the kerb-stone
> on the empty road, and a yellow, panic-stricken,
> bear clutched,
> for the impossible move
> across
> to the school bus
> and the day's nightmare.[3]

At the very least, we owe it to our pupils that school should not be a daily nightmare. Neither should school be a nightmare for teachers and headteachers — as, alas, it too often is. I quote the poem in order to make these obvious points. Further, the poem introduces Part One of this paper, which begins with a nightmare vision of contemporary Britain. The nightmare is presented in a way which will become clear after the first few lines.

The case for no confidence

The 1990s began, before the end of their first year, with an event which at the time had all the appearance of being the most momentous setback, perhaps indeed the most devastating tragedy, which our nation had ever had the misfortune to experience. I refer to the departure from our shores, through barely believable cowardice, treachery and short-sightedness, of leadership and inspiration, order and decency, vigour and purpose. It seemed for a while that we no longer had any national vision.

And yet the genius of our nation — of our race — is such that men in this land did quite swiftly recover from the tragedy of autumn 1990, and in the course of the ensuing decade did continue steadfast, and vigorous and faithful, in the new pathways which had been so boldly planned, and so bravely pioneered, in the 1980s.

In this speech now in autumn 1999, I wish to look back over our principal achievements during the decade which is about to close, and to highlight the main components of our success. I hope and intend in this way to clarify and to consolidate the policy priorities for our race in the century, or rather — to speak more frankly and less modestly — in the millennium, which is now about to begin.

The first essential component of our success lies in a piece of legislation which has been so extraordinarily effective in moulding men's behaviour that most people nowadays are unaware that it even exists. The Policy Discourse and Semantics Act 1992 had, let us recall, two main aspects. On the one hand, there was PONST — Prohibition of Non-Sanctioned Terminology. This enabled us to introduce Relaxation of Restraints on Crime and the Subversion Detection (RRCSD), but not what our critics and opponents, in the absence of PONST, would have mischievously referred to as 'the use of torture'. Similarly we could introduce Enterprise and Accommodation Units for the Unemployed (EAUUs), but not 'workhouses', and Keystage Three Identification of Non-Academic Citizens (KS3INAC) but not 'losla' — not 'lowering of the school leaving age'.

The other main aspect of the Policy Discourse and Semantics Act was the outlawing of certain words and phrases which had had a certain vogue in the 1980s but which would only foster discontent if we allowed them to remain any longer in daily use in policy-making and decision-making — thus we finally rid the public vocabulary of 'anti-racism' and 'anti-sexism', also of all other similarly un-English words formed with the prefix 'anti', and of ludicrous but harmful phrases such as 'sex discrimination', 'positive action', 'equal opportunities', and 'chairperson'; further, we successfully defended the English language against various nonsensical words coined by European bureaucrats, for example 'harmonisation', 'asylum-seeker' and 'xenophobia'.

Other achievements of the decade include the abolition of the Race Relations Act and of the Sex Discrimination Act in 1993, the Guestworker and Immigrant Redefinition Act 1994, the Guestworker and Immigrant Dispersal and Assimilation Act 1995, the Guestworker and Immigrant Humane Repatriation Act 1996, the Women as Homemakers Act 1997, and the Christianity Beliefs and Morality Act 1998.

In the field of education the decade saw the abolition of teacher training institutions in 1992, of Her Majesty's Inspectorate in 1993 and of local authorities in 1994. We were very fortunate, from 1994 onwards, to be able to put all teacher training and re-education, and all monitoring, inspection and evaluation, into the hands of the former British Army of the Rhine, now known as the Benchmarks, Assessment, Ousting and Re-education service. In the writing and dissemination of inspection reports BAOR has been much helped over the years by its partnership with Saatchi and Saatchi in relation to good schools, and with the *Mail on Sunday* in relation to bad ones.

I am proud to announce today that just over 60 per cent of the population is now being educated at good schools: 25 per cent at fully independent schools, and 35 per cent at grant-maintained schools; this is a remarkable achievement. Teachers at these schools are so well paid that they do not need to join trade unions. Fewer than 40 per cent of the pupils in our schools are so lacking in intelligence that they need to leave school at the end of Keystage Three; this too is a remarkable achievement.

In the course of the decade we have magnificently succeeded in removing, from positions of power and influence, all people with 'progressive' or 'caring' ideas about education. I can illustrate this achievement with an interesting statistic. Some eight years ago, in September 1991, there was a conference entitled 'Accountability with Confidence' at, as it was in those days called, the University of Cambridge. Before coming here today, I consulted the National Subversives and Undesirables Computer Index, and I can tell you this. Of the people who were at that conference in 1991, five per cent are now sadly dead; 10 per cent are in detention or psychiatric hospital; 30 per cent are unemployed. Of the remaining 55 per cent, 25 per cent no longer have any connection with education. Of those who do still work in or with education, only five per cent have higher status or greater influence now than in 1991. I am happy to reassure everybody here today that those persons are, of course, kept under very strict surveillance.

There is still, in education and in society, some unfinished business. We still need to expand the police force, for example, and to build more prisons and psychiatric hospitals; we still need to implement fully the Eugenics Act 1997, for it is still the case that intelligent people are not having enough children, and that the lower classes are having too many; and women, alas, though bless them, are still allowed to vote in local elections.

But matters such as these are basically straightforward. There are no grounds for pessimism, concern or anxiety. On the contrary, the future for our race, in view of the recent past, is — is it not? — gloriously hopeful.

Lurid and melodramatic though this is, the nightmare can be presented entirely soberly, indeed scientifically. There are eight propositions altogether. Six are encoded into the content of the piece, and two are encoded into the choice of genre. First, the prediction is that there will be greater inequality in 1999 than there is in 1991. That is, there will be a higher percentage of children and adults living in households where the income is less than half the national average. (At present, incidentally, more than a fifth of all children live in such households, and there are 3.8 million such households altogether.)

Second, increasing levels of inequality will disproportionately disadvantage certain ethnic minority communities. Asian and Black people will be even more represented than at present amongst those who are living in the poorest households, as defined above; more will be represented than at present in the least desirable and serviceable housing stock; and more represented amongst those who are unemployed. Third, women will be no less represented in the poorest households than at present, and no more represented than at present in positions of senior management.

Fourth, it is being predicted that it will be found that education has not made a significant difference to the life-chances and career prospects of (a) people in the poorest households, (b) most Black and Asian people, and (c) women, when the pattern in 1999 is compared with the pattern in 1991. Fifth, there will be little or no government policy focused on reducing inequality, and few or no resources. At least some of the policy discourse in the 1990s, and at least some of the specific decisions which are made about resources, will actually increase inequality. Sixth, there will be a measurable decline in civil liberties and human rights.

The seventh and eighth propositions encoded into the nightmare are expressed through the choice of genre — the use of great exaggeration, and the presentation of an apparently unstoppable dystopia. Seventh, then, it is being claimed that the vast majority of people do not know and do not care that our society is characterised by increasing inequality, and that the inequality is disproportionately working to the disadvantage of Asian and Black people, and of women. Eighth, the nightmare suggests that those who do know and care feel that they are powerless to do anything about this situation — they feel that they are de-skilled, disempowered, marginalised, paralysed. They feel they are in a nightmare. They cannot find within themselves the confidence of that child at Chalkhill School: 'I am an egg ready to hatch, I bring with me life'.

The case against no confidence

It is time now for the defending counsel, so to speak, to take the stand. The first task is to show or argue that the pessimist's account of the world is not warranted by the objective facts. This will include, and will start with, the casting of doubts on the pessimist's reliability and motivation. Let us imagine that the defending advocate opens the case with a set of rhetorical questions, as follows:

You are, Pessimist, fearful and critical of what you regard as the 'new' political Right. I put it to you that your actual knowledge and firsthand experiences of the Right are much too narrow for you to be a reliable witness. Your view, if I understand you correctly, is that compared with the average right-wing politician of your acquaintance, the average lager-swilling National-Front-supporting skinhead whom you know is a person of high moral principles, moderate opinions, generous expectations, soft speech, and gentle manners. Come on, Pessimist, come on. Do not extrapolate from your own narrow experience.

Moreover, and much more seriously, I put it to you that you are — I use the term quite technically, you understand — paranoid. Did you, I wonder, see *The Trial* by Franz Kafka, adapted by Steven Berkoff, which played during summer 1991 at the National Theatre? The play was a marvellous portrayal and enactment of paranoia, and reminded me in a whole range of respects, Pessimist, of yourself. Joseph K, the main character, feels that the whole of society is accusing him, persecuting him, imprisoning and constricting him, literally throttling and murdering him. Berkoff's stage production showed vividly that Joseph K's society is peopled only, however, by projections and externalisations from within himself. His nightmare, his sense of oppression and powerlessness, has its roots in his own personality, not in surrounding society.

It is some sort of inner change which you require, Pessimist, not a programme of political action. 'The Right', as you call it, is a figment of your imagination. Your task, which if I may say so is basically a kind of spiritual task, is to reach the serenity of Prospero at the end of *The Tempest* when he says, as it were, 'This thing of Rightness I acknowledge mine'. Take back your projections, Pessimist, take them back into your own self or spirit or soul, and deal with them there.

For what you call the Right is a coalition of very many different groupings and trends. It is not a homogeneous entity, and no one group is dominant. Certainly what might be called the authoritarian, nationalist or fascist tendency is not in the ascendancy, and you are making a serious error of judgement in supposing that it is. Other far more significant tendencies on the Right include the libertarian, decentralising and free-market tendency, and this has given at least as much attention to concepts of civil liberty, and personal accountability, empowerment and autonomy, as anyone on the Left; and the One Nation tendency, which is genuinely concerned with order and security, and a decent life for all; and what may be termed 'the small c conservative' tendency.

The outlook of this last tendency is captured by the legendary remark of a senior civil servant to a cabinet minister: 'Change? You want change? Aren't things bad enough already?' The small c conservative tendency puts emphasis on conserving traditions of due process, rule of law, rational debate, courteous discourse. Conserving is a matter of maintaining democracy in good repair, and passing it on to the next generation. This is not, Pessimist, an ignoble activity, and it is one which is far more likely than any programme of yours to prevent the emergence of a totalitarian state.

You fail to see the real debates, specifically in the civil service and in local government. What is the right balance between individual action and social action, and between voluntary and statutory bodies? How do we balance decentralisation and accountability? What pluralist models of welfare and caring can we appropriately develop, as distinct from state-monopoly models? How can we provide and develop forms of motivation amongst government employees which are genuinely client-centred, and which act as models for 'enlightened' (as distinct from merely self-interested) action in society more widely? What models of co-operation and co-ordination between specialist professionals and concerned lay people can be developed? How do we evaluate market and non-market ways of allocating scarce resources? How do we shift British culture and the education system away from damaging and simplistic views of technology, engineering and science, and of the real nature of economic and industrial enterprise? In what ways has municipal socialism failed by its own (its own, Pessimist, please note) lights and values? And how culturally do we apply that old twofold maxim that 'equality without differentiation is bad equality, and differentiation without equality is bad differentiation'? How do we achieve both social cohesion on the one hand and genuine pluralism in private life on the other — for example, how do we protect liberalism and diversity, but not fall into the kinds of internal conflict which have been plunging Eastern European countries into various kinds of civil war and disorder?

These are the debates of our time, Pessimist, and it is to these that you should be contributing. They are contests in both senses: there are major issues at stake, and what is required is con-testing, a joint collaborative enquiry into viable ways ahead.

There is far more good will in our society, Pessimist, and far more respect for due process and the rule of law, than your scenario implies. For example, we can surely rely much more on the good sense, responsibility and rationality of school governors than you seem to think. Also, you misjudge the strength of the oppressed. You seem to have no faith in the power of disadvantaged people to organise and defend themselves. Your scenario of increasing power-lessness for those who are already in positions of weakness and poverty takes no account of people's capacity to look after them-selves. Do you really think, for example, that women in this country would permit anything remotely similar to your scenario so far as gender equality is concerned? Do you really think that Muslim communities in Bradford and Tower Hamlets, and elsewhere, would permit the assaults on Islam which your scenario would involve?

This lack of faith in the oppressed implies that you are not really, as you claim, their friend. Fortunately, they do not need you. I rest my case.

What then shall we do?

A teenager writes:

> There is so much going on inside me.
> I am mixed up, I am confused.
> I have no name, no country, no home, no colour.
> I am ME, but who am I?
> Is to be oneself enough, or does one need more?[4]

As we adults work to become effective, wrestling with the cases for and against pessimism, we have to stay in contact with the different, but analogous, passions and heartaches of the young, as they too work to become effective. For it is to them, from the perspective of history, that we are accountable: they are going to enter into our work, our acting, and they are going to use our work and our acting as resources for themselves.

I shall briefly suggest seven sets of principles which could appro-priately guide our actions. They are offered as a kind of package, in the sense that each needs to be accompanied, sharpened and strength-ened by each of the others. I am seeking to make explicit now various points which have so far been implicit in this chapter. Before listing and discussing the seven points briefly in turn, I should like again to recall a young person's perspective. Here is one of the people to whom we are accountable, and for whom we have to provide, and in our own persons to be, resources:

> Oi! Paki! Wotcha doin' in our country?
> Go back to where you belong.
>
> I hold my head up high and proud
> And walk on with dignity.
> How long can I walk on?
> How long can I ignore?

> The anger inside me burns red, dark red.
> How I'd like to tear them apart . . .
> But instead I hold my anger.[5]

First we need what might be called, following a suggestion by Salman Rushdie, the principle of hybridity. In a piece entitled *In Good Faith* Salman Rushdie wrote as follows:

> If *The Satanic Verses* is anything, it is a migrant's-eye view of the world. It is written from the very experience of uprooting, disjuncture and metamorphosis (slow or rapid, painful or pleasurable) that is the migrant condition, and from which, I believe, can be derived a metaphor for all humanity . . .
>
> *The Satanic Verses* celebrates hybridity, impurity, intermingling the transformation that comes from new and unexpected combinations of human beings, cultures, ideas, politics, movies, songs. It rejoices in mongrelisation and fears the absolutism of the Pure.
>
> Mélange, hotchpotch, a bit of this and a bit of that is *how newness enters the world*. It is the great possibility that mass migration gives the world.[6]

We have to embrace impurity and mixing, Rushdie is maintaining, and suggesting therefore amongst other things that our only health lies in being ideologically unsound. It follows that we need to listen to and learn from those with whom we disagree, and that we need also to be in alliance with some of them. Together we need to gather, deploy and use resources — finance, energy, time, expertise, communication networks and platforms, contacts and relationships. One key alliance in this respect is between professionals and non-specialists, specifically between teachers and parents.

Second, there is what might be called the principle of ethical resistance. The task is to find ways of resisting which are not merely as unprincipled and unethical as the strategies and operations of those whom we oppose. Otherwise, there is no real gain; the likelihood is merely, as Yeats said in a famous brief reflection, that beggars will change places whilst the lash goes on:

> Hurrah for revolution and more cannon-shot!
> A beggar upon horseback lashes a beggar on foot.
> Hurrah for revolution and cannon come again!
> The beggars have changed places, but the lash goes on.[7]

This is a pragmatic point in the first instance rather than a principled one: the wrong means actually prevent you from reaching the right ends. There is in addition the need to avoid demonising the enemy. Certainly the press has demonised Asian and Black politicians and leaders in Britain in recent years, and the onslaught on 'trendy', 'progressive' teachers has similarly been characterised by a demonising tendency. But that is no excuse for the rest of us to demonise the Right. The avoidance of demonising has two aspects: the acknowledgement of faults and failings within one's own ranks, and the parallel acknowledgement of sincerity and insight amongst one's opponents.

Third, there is the importance of narrative — the making and keeping of accounts. What we are up against is a body of narrative: for example, racism and nationalism are kept alive through narratives as well as through structures, and we need our own oppositional narratives in order to deal with them. Racism has a grand narrative, or myth, and then countless small episodes and anecdotes which both embody the main myth and also help to vivify and perpetuate it. (Similarly a religion, for example, has a grand narrative, and then a mass of history, biography, fable, parable, legend, wisdom tale, chronicle, and so on.) One of our minimal duties is to tell stories and accounts about our resistance to the worst lunacies and threats in the Education Reform Act, and about both our successes and defeats. Some of the stories need to be about our own faults, failings, weaknesses and internal quarrels — though we need to be careful, of course, as to where exactly we tell these, and who exactly may be eavesdropping.

We need true stories (though bearing in mind that marvellous Russian saying: 'he lied like an eye-witness'), and also tales of the imagination. Our stories should not only foster opposition to other myths but should also be strengthening and illumining as we each of us tell and construct our own life-story. Just as a religion has a grand narrative and then lots of much smaller episodes which fit into it, so too does each of us have a single story into which we try to fit all the smaller happenings of our lives. The single story has a beginning in birth to that one mother, in that one household and family tradition, to that one constellation of language and accent, in that one place, at that one historical moment. It has its own distinctive and unique middle in our work and loves. One day each life story has an end. We need stories — myths and folktales as well as true accounts — to help us hold the beginnings, middles and ends of our lives together. Without them we shall not have hope: yes, to lose stories is to lose hope, but conversely to construct and cherish stories is to maintain hope.

'Human beings', writes Gabriel Garcia Marquez, 'are not born once and for all on the day their mothers give birth to them, but life obliges them over and over again to give birth to themselves'.[8] The construction and sharing of stories helps us, daily, to give birth to ourselves.

Fourth, it follows, the whole field of arts education is critically important. The arts confront the reductionism and mechanistic philistinism in the Education Reform Act, and in each individual school, as also in society much more widely, and they can help fashion and hold the balance between cohesion and pluralism. In schools they are absolutely central in what has been called LMV — the local management of values. Arts education needs to be imbued with the principle of hybridity, sketched with the quotation from Salman Rushdie above, and to be concerned with the construction and sharing of narrative.

Fifth, there is the importance of the individual school, and the individual body of governors. One of the most exciting and potentially liberating aspects of the new legislation is the greater autonomy for each separate institution. 'Governor training', as the term is, has been called one of the most remarkable programmes of adult education ever mounted in this country, with very many thousands of people becoming involved in careful, practical and localised debates about — to summarise very grandly — the good life and the good society. The arguments explored in this chapter are being handled and moulded in each and every separate school.

Sixth, there is the principle of passion. The word has two meanings, suffering and anger, and implies also love. The connection between the two meanings is that we frequently feel anger when we suffer, particularly when the suffering is out of all proportion to our deserts. Thus there is the bitterness and anger when we are crushed, rejected or ignored, or when people close and dear to us are crushed or ignored. We have to avoid using our anger as, for example, Joseph K uses his anger in *The Trial* — to populate the world with demons and enemies from out of his own nightmare inner world, and to attribute all power and initiative to them. At best, the energy in anger can be transmuted into the energy of love, and the energy of making things — making stories, making cases, bringing new life into the world.

Seventh, there is the principle of downwards accountability. The parent is accountable to the child, and the teacher to the learner. So is the educational administrator, the college lecturer, the adviser or inspector, the member of the education committee. And the present is accountable to the future. Accountability involves both telling and listening to stories; and, having listened, re-telling. Rather similarly, incidentally, judges and advocates are accountable to a jury. And a writer is accountable to a readership, and a speaker or lecturer to an audience.

As a way of illustrating the ideas and principles in the final section of this chapter, I should like to quote one last piece of poetry about children and young people, and about the accountability which we all have towards them. The poem is set, very appropriately, in a school classroom. It's by Fiona Norris, and its title is *Classroom Politics*. It begins as follows:

They will not forgive us
These girls
Sitting in serried rows
Hungry for attention
Like shelves of unread books,
If we do not
Make the world new for them,
Teach them to walk
Into the possibilities
Of their own becoming
Confident in their exploring.[9]

An agenda is beautifully sketched and focused here for careful discussions and debates involving, in each separate school, teachers, parents and governors. Such discussions and debates will surely lead to more children and young people being able to say what that child at Chalkhill school in north London said, and perhaps too to a world being made and maintained which is fit for them to live and say it in: 'I am an egg ready to hatch. I bring with me life.'

References

[1]   From *Children's Self-Worth Poems*, compiled by Stephen Delsol, Brent Education Department, 1990.
[2]   *Equality and Excellence*, Brent Education Department, 1991.
[3]   Bill Allchin, *A Turmoil of Fragile Hearts*, Sarsen Press, 1989.
[4]   By Jenneba Sie Jalloh, quoted in *Drum, Talk and Dub*, Brent Education Department, 1990.
[5]   By Tania Ahsan, quoted in *Drum, Talk and Dub*, Brent Education Department, 1990.
[6]   Salman Rushdie, *In Good Faith*, first published in *The Independent on Sunday*, 4 February 1990, pp. 18-20.
[7]   W. B. Yeats, 'The Great Day', in *Selected Poetry*, Macmillan, 1962, p. 190.
[8]   Gabriel Garcia Marquez, *Love in the Time of Cholera*, 1985, p. 165 of the Penguin Books edition.
[9]   From 'Classroom Politics' by Fiona Norris, in *Yesterday Today Tomorrow*, compiled by Jane Leggett and Ros Moger, ILEA English Centre, 1987, p. 21.

Note

Earlier versions of this chapter were presented at two conferences organised in summer 1991 by, respectively, the University of Warwick and the National Union of Teachers. The version printed here reflects discussions at those conferences as well as, more especially and more extensively, discussions at the conference at Robinson College, Cambridge, in September 1991.

9.2 The uses of diversity
Michael Day

Accountability extends beyond any immediate system. A wider context suggests sterner challenges, though the understandable temptation is to shut as much of that out as possible and get on with managing the corner of the world more directly under our control.

But this will not work, or at least not for very long. Confidence in our future will depend on successfully tackling the inequalities and stresses which lie behind the current turbulence and working at some framework of accountability that responds to diverse interests. There is all the difference between pre-occupation with one sector, and managing that responsibly in the broader context to help shape wider change.

So there is a need to escape from the limits we impose on ourselves by becoming trapped into a mono-culture which blocks off the experience of others' traditions. Failure of imagination makes us reluctant to reshape our institutions and systems to the needs of a diverse multi-racial society. It is much safer to stay within the bounds of traditions and styles that are familiar and reassuring. We avoid having to contend with the uncertainty of surrendering control and allowing other cultures to permeate our world. But we may grow to recognise that in imposing constraints on others, requiring that they accommodate themselves to our ways, we are denying ourselves so much. Owing allegiance to one set of values, one source of accountability, may seem to provide the security of the predictable but it ensures neither capacity to contend with the unexpected nor confidence to deal with the tensions of conflicting pressures and loyalties.

A clear system of accountability may prove to be too one-dimensional to handle conflicting obligations. Challenge to one neat, predictable frame of reference may be resisted by us because it threatens our security — the world of beliefs and developed defences we have come to rely on. But if that world is reinforced, consolidated into a fixed position, cannot give and absorb pressure and thereby adapt, it will eventually be confronted by an onslaught of new thinking, of power systems which crush it. Accountability to one set of values, one system or closed community prevents adaptation. Confidence of the kind I am talking of, the capacity to react creatively to a changing environment and acquire greater resilience and inner strength; that authority and command can surely come only by positioning oneself securely in relation to a complex range of experiences and possibilities and being able to depend on an institutional, professional culture to sustain the person and the values.

Having different sets of accountabilities may leave you bewildered and uncertain, overwhelmed and not knowing where to turn or where duty lies. Yet it may also be the opportunity to respond in a way which expresses your own responsibility and is therefore liberating.

Accountability to a pluralist society calls for a radically new management of our institutions. It cannot be met by requiring diversity to accommodate itself to a pre-ordained scheme. It will not be enough to make small adjustments on the margins. Power which is not legitimised by proper accountability is doomed and has no right to barter with what it does not properly own. Relevance to an ethnically and religiously diverse society, a broader, more open Europe and a world of easier movement and interchange means not simply introducing some programme of cultural awareness in an obviously multi-racial area, but bringing that wider dimension to bear on the whole curriculum — not tacked on at the edge, making some additional provision, but reorganising the mainstream. An accountability restricted to one part of the community may proudly claim long-standing presence and proprietorial rights but it is flawed and imprisons those whose interests it reckons to protect. Responsiveness to the needs of minority groupings, whether in the field of education or any other service, is bound to enhance the quality of provision overall, but that only if it is seen as a widening of accountability — and not abandoning one client group for another. Much of the controversy around multi-cultural education and other programmes for minority communities arises from a perception that privilege and attention is being transferred to the detriment of a more 'eligible' majority. It is a very tall order to convince parents that curriculum time directed at human rights issues or appreciation of other cultures is not at the expense of the narrower and shorter-term academic achievement by which their children and the school's success will be assessed.

If we cannot rely on people willingly conceding to the more pressing needs of others and recognising that disparity will cause stress and in time threaten the stability of the whole, we must introduce machinery to bring that about. The intervention of law makes explicit and statutory an accountability which, to command the support of the community, must represent justice and reflect an acknowledged overall authority. Its framing declares an expectation and lays responsibilities on citizens. Simply, in the case of seat belts, and with more complexity in the fraught field of race, the formality of enforcement machinery guarantees the protection of the vulnerable and accountability to due process strengthens the resolve of waverers.

But formalising accountability through legal, organisational or political structures gives no guarantee of quality. It may clarify who is responsible for what and give a possibly spurious impression of efficiency. But unless that is matched by an internalised commitment to improved performance — a combination of professional values and emotional and moral force — there will be mismatch and tension but little creativity. People may formally comply but effectively frustrate. Confidence will be undermined by a feeling of being overmanaged and constrained, of being required to make professional talents available as a marketable commodity rather than cherished and accommodated within a sensitive system. It is questionable whether the local management of schools, the removal of accountability to local education authorities and the rather ambiguous financial stewardship and employer status of governing bodies will encourage innovation, diversity, a more rigorous and successful school regime or lock teaching skills into narrower confines. Will financial accountability discourage risk and creativity in the interests of measurable academic output and the need to attract parent 'customers'? Some constraints of accountability are more calculated to reassure those who carry overall political responsibility than give confidence to managers and practitioners. My impression is that the kind of bureaucratic accountability demanded by the new system, emphasis on performance indicators and pushing financial management close to professional delivery leaves heads and teachers unconfident of the support and cover they will receive and likely to be cautious, inhibited and undermined, not feeling part of a total system whose values and professionalism are shared. There is a feeling that the balance between professional and financial and political accountability has been upset — the 'bottom line' becomes the main criterion. Professionalism may sometimes be traded as a debased coinage but the essential components — knowledge base, practitioner skills, exercise of responsible personal judgement and reference to an institution which codifies and controls practice — represent an accountability which ties in with individual commitment and therefore enhances esteem and confidence. We seem to be in danger of sacrificing that precious linkage just as we have largely lost the pride and discipline of guilds and trades. Practitioners may become units of skilled labour whose accountability is contractual and suffers all the uncertainty of fluctuating markets and political vagaries. We lose the safeguard of authoritative and powerful associations, and there is less investment in the kind of monitoring arrangements which overlay formal management lines of accountability with bold delegation, decentralisation and lateral accountability between professionals. It makes no pretence of professional autonomy, which in an accountable system is a myth, but creates a climate of trust and gives individuals scope to reconcile potentially conflicting accountabilities and acquire self-confidence.

That is the proper exercise of discretion in a professional role: holding the tension between different sets of obligations and struggling to achieve as close a match as possible between personal values and contractual demands. The great problem in many professional settings — medicine, social work, for instance, as well as education — is that practitioners have experienced an oppressive over-emphasis on contractual, financial accountability, which has demoralised and undermined esteem. Output measures have been made the criteria of success. That is questionable: the process itself has value.

This is not to suggest that professionals should brook no interference. They are not free-standing virtuoso performers, but work within systems which must mobilise their skills and introduce a system of organisational accountability. That in itself lends security. The challenge is to be sensitive to the proper interplay between obligations, so that excesses which may arise from an over-emphasis on one line of accountability can be held in check. But no system will last if it relies on one source of power. The weight of political, contractual demand has to be resisted and balanced by strengthening professional interests, allowing the exercise of individual responsibility and the influence of professional values. It has to be sustained by the collaborative commitment to shared aims by those who contribute to the overall task. Only then will the enterprise as a whole have integrity and those who work within it feel good about themselves.

9.3   Afterword
John Bazalgette

When people come together to produce a book about accountability in education there are many things running through their minds and hearts. Perhaps if I write down some of those that are in mine it will help people to reflect on the book as a whole as well as on individual contributions.

A gallimaufry of topics

There have been plenty of issues talked about: values, beliefs, teachers and their relations with society, resourcing and effectiveness, concern for ethnic minorities, parents and their relations with school. People have asked, 'accountability for what? For teaching? For learning?' — these are clearly not the same. We can all think of examples which demonstrate that what was learned at school is not the same as what was taught; most of us will remember things about the characters who taught us — things we learned from them — but the subjects they taught us have ebbed away on the tide of time. Much attention has been given to who is involved in the school, the class, the community and how they are accountable — or not. There has been talk of decisions, resources, measuring, assessment and evaluation.

Two popular ideas have been 'partnership' and 'leadership': no one opposes these good things, though I am not sure what they mean by them or even if some people mean the same thing by them, even when they appear to be in agreement.

The notion of accountability is one about which it is not easy to disagree. It commands at least polite expressions of assent. How real will these assents be? Will they stand up to the harsh winds of the storms of racial prejudice, deprivation, oppression, poverty, underachievement, contraction and inequality which the Chairman of the Commission for Racial Equality has written about?

What happens to children in all of this? Do they slip in and out of the discussions, sometimes fully on stage, sometimes lost behind the scenery, sometimes waiting in the wings or peeping round the tabs? I have no doubt that they are in everyone's minds, though often unreferred to. But that is the trouble: our silence about them can mean that at critical times we may leave them out of account and unwittingly base decisions on our own interests.

The social, political and statutory contexts

We have to face up to the kind of world in which today's pupils as men and women in due course will have to survive and for which they will have to take responsibility: they will vote, work, create wealth, bring up children, take responsibility for their families, towns, counties, country and perhaps more. They already live in a world where some are part of an underclass, while others are part of a ruling class. But those young people are in the class that they are because the society they are growing up in accepts to a greater or less degree (since we have not had a revolution about it yet) the differences that are thus reflected. Will all this erupt violently like we hear about in the Balkans? Or in some other form?

The fact is that teachers inevitably pass on to their pupils the grasp they have of the realities of the context. The better the grasp they have of those realities, the better they will prepare their pupils for participation in it in their turn. Through their own sense of accountability, teachers can be encouraged to link what they do now with the futures of those in their charge.

There has been considerable discussion about the various pieces of legislation under which education is now provided, which have strengthened the notion of accountability. Whatever anyone's personal political position, it is worth noting that something along the same lines would have been introduced by any government of whatever political colour, because of rising concern in society about the effectiveness of the schooling our children have been receiving. There are speeches given by Shirley Williams in the late 1970s which, if unattributed, could have been taken as being Kenneth Baker's.

The model of the market place

However, what is distinctive to the present government has been the way it has suggested that the relation between a school and its turbulent context could be interpreted. It has proposed the idea that this can be done through the concept of the 'market place', which has provided a model for thinking based on the relationship between customers and suppliers. We have been asked to think of schools in the same way as we think about Marks and Spencer, British Gas and Esso. By getting Coopers Lybrand (a firm of accountants) to propose ways of assessing schools and their performance, that model has been even more deeply planted in our thinking and has been around all over the country for some years now, even in the thoughts and talk of those who find that the model jars with them.

Accountability: giving an account

It is perhaps one of the great travesties of language during the past decade or more that 'accountability' has been given that narrow, market-place connotation.

It has become associated with financial control, cost-benefit, performance indicators, cash limits, income and expenditure, value for money and all the finance-based thinking that goes with them. There is nothing the matter with that, and it is arguable that over the years education, social work, health, the penal system and even the church have failed to attend properly to accounting for this side of their affairs.

But if we pause to reflect, we must be struck by the fact that the root of the word is *'account'*: to give an account is *'to tell the story* . . .'[1]. Thus, if I ask a teacher to give me an account of a child's learning, I am asking for the teacher to tell me the story of what new ideas, knowledge or understanding that child has gained; I shall be interested in their attitudes to the world they are growing up in; are they curious about it or about themselves and their reaction to it? How is this boy or girl changing?

If I ask a teacher to tell me the story of a class, I am asking for a description of the culture and performance of a group: what can these children do together? Under what circumstance do they strive to achieve with a sense of giving support to each other and when do they compete rivalrously and destructively? What kind of moral norms have they established amongst themselves? Do they feel that the resources they have been given to work with are theirs of right, or do they feel they have them in trust? What grasp have they of 'quality' in what they do? How do they relate to their teacher or anyone else in authority?

A call for a suitable language

These considerations at the level of the child and the class — which can be raised to the levels of the school, the education authority and a society's education system as a whole — draw our attention to the need for a language with which to tell the particular story we wish to have recounted.

This brings into view a way of thinking about what is taught at school. After all, what is any subject but a different way of focusing a story about mankind in its environment? History is the story of a family, tribe, community, nation or race in relation to achievements and setbacks over time. Geography is the story of mankind in the context of place: physical, climatic or social. Science is the story of the structure of matter and the forces which affect its behaviour.

Each of these stories has developed its own applied language which focuses upon those features to which it wishes to direct particular attention. This is where English and mathematics are interesting in relation to all other subjects because they provide the fundamental languages upon which all other subjects draw to tell their own stories.

If we as a society wish to make teachers and schools more account-able for what goes on within the walls of their classrooms, halls and playgrounds, we need to work with them to develop a language which focuses the kind of story we need to hear.

So, as we read the contributions to this book, what kinds of language do we find their stories are couched in? Is it a language that puts us in touch with those real boys and girls who inhabit the classrooms up and down our land? Do we find ourselves filled with confidence by what those stories tell us? Do the tellers of the stories have difficulties to recount — ordeals even? Do we feel that these are people who can carry the responsibility for taking action within the situation or do they seem to be running away, speaking as victims of forces beyond their control, passing the buck? Put together, these papers represent something like the whole of this society's provision for children: a parent, teachers of children at different stages, heads, those responsible for quality, for the administration of an area, of political direction and the longer-term vision.

Confidence

I expect that much of what is written will convey things about having confidence in a personal sense. People will write and speak about how they felt as individuals. I note that Susan Heightman, writing as a mother, says she felt happy and accountable, but she did not feel confident on the birth of her daughter. Others suggest that as teach-ers, heads, administrators and politicians, they have doubted their capacity to discharge their responsibilities as adequately as they would have liked. Nevertheless, the fact is that not only have they accepted the jobs for which they are paid or to which they have been elected, but they have been willing to contribute their experience to this book. They may have felt they lacked confidence, but they had enough to do this!

To reflect upon accountability is also to reflect upon the feelings of those who appointed you to be a head, class teacher, director of education or whatever. Remember that people are removed from office as a result of a vote of no confidence, which is about how other people feel about you, not how you feel about yourself.

What was received upon appointment was the authority of the role. Thus part of one's confidence derives from one's understanding about the authority conferred upon one in taking up the role and one's ability to exercise that authority. So personal confidence is also about confidence in the structures which conferred that authority. Were you given terms of reference? Did you understand them? Have you been given the resources for the job, including the finance, time, the status, appropriately qualified staff, and the buildings? Without adequate resources you could not have the power you need to do the job. In John Whiting's play, *Saint's Day*, a house party refuses to take note of the postman who comes in to warn them of impending disaster because he had not the status in their eyes to be worth taking note of. Perhaps some of those who can see problems ahead for our present society have no more status than that postman as they give their warnings: they too will go unheeded even when they warn of the consequences of so important a matter as education.

Attitudes to structures: past and present

In the past, before the legislation which has clarified the accountability of local authorities, governors, heads and teachers, there was an attitude which was common in many maintained schools. This was that every successful school developed tactics and strategies by which to beat the 'system': it was understood that the local authority and its officers had resources, especially money, usually hidden in various pockets which officers could defend and deploy within the policies advanced by elected members. Talented heads and officers who were effective in bringing about change in the bureaucracy, knew how to 'beat the system'.

A major consequence of the new statutory arrangements is that it no longer makes sense to try to 'beat the system'. All those within the system are now challenged to *make the system work*. This has major implications for how one understands accountability.

A final thought: representation

I find that something different is thrown up in my mind by taking these ideas a bit further. Accountability links me to other people; structures define who those people are and what the accountability is about. This means that I am therefore a representative of others, acting for them in carrying forward things they cannot do for themselves for whatever reason. I may act on behalf of parents who wish to use a school and its teachers to enable them to discharge their responsibility to educate their child, because they recognise that in today's technological world very few parents are equipped to fulfil such a responsibility; I may act on behalf of elected members who hammer out a policy for a community but need professional people to put it to work; I may be a headteacher who cannot teach everything in my school so need to deploy others to work with children in classes on my behalf.

If I reflect on my accountability to the children — downwards accountability — I am in a sense the representative of their futures: standing in the position of introducing them to the selves they will become in several years time, as workers, parents, undergraduates and voters.

In today's climate I need to enquire of myself what will it mean to represent? One of the papers included here (by Maggie Pringle) answers this by pointing out that to represent someone means to *embody* them, to take them and their interests into myself and reflect what that means. As a head considers what she embodies she has to have the qualities which enable her to carry in herself both those people who disagree with each other and those with whom she may herself disagree. To be the head and to be accountable to all those involved, she must sustain in her person all the stress and contradiction that entails. Her stature and competence as a head will reflect the span of what she can hold inside herself before the differences between them become too much and she can no longer tolerate the strain. The richness and range of opportunities in that school will stem directly from that capacity in the headteacher.

This is a very different thing from another kind of embodying which another writer (Christine Webb) notes — the embodiment of lists. The danger of the National Curriculum is that it can lead to accountability being about the embodiment of lists — the accountability of the petty bureaucrat, the restrictor of humanity. The fantasy is that if I fulfil the terms of a list given me by someone else then I have discharged my accountability. But in the world of learning, changing, maturing children the prospect of that kind of accountability is appalling. By contrast, the 'embodying of people' kind of accountability is a spur for learning, vitality and maturity which can lay the foundation for a society of the future of which we can be proud.

However, we have to face the fact that with today's individualism such a form of accountability is not easy to adopt. It requires maturity, skills and attitudes which are rare rather than common. It will need the kinds of mutuality of confidence between persons and structures which the market-place model — represented by the bleeping automated check-out system, based on efficient listing — tends to undermine rather than to foster. Yet, paradoxically, what those who support that legislation (and most of us do) are looking for are the very things that model destroys.

This book has invited the reader to wander through the maze and to consider whether or not the ideas about accountability contained in it give confidence in the future of our society. Perhaps the few pointers laid here will help in that consideration.

Note

1   The *Concise Oxford Dictionary* (eighth edition 1990) begins its defini-
    tion of account with the words 'narration or description'. It is probably
    significant that the illustration which the dictionary immediately offers
    is 'gave a long account of the ordeal'! It may also be an encouraging sign
    of our times that the third edition (1934) opens with a much more
    financial definition.